READING WITH THE MASORETES
The Exegetical Utility of Masoretic Accent Patterns

GlossaHouse Dissertation Series Volume 8
GDS 8

READING WITH THE MASORETES
THE EXEGETICAL UTILITY OF MASORETIC ACCENT PATTERNS

MARCUS A. LEMAN

GLOSSAHOUSE
WILMORE, KY
WWW.GLOSSAHOUSE.COM

READING WITH THE MASORETES:
THE EXEGETICAL UTILITY OF MASORETIC ACCENT PATTERNS
© GlossaHouse, LLC, 2019

All rights reserved. No part of this book may be reproduced or transmitted in any form or by any means, electronic or mechanical, including photocopying or recording, or by means of any information storage or retrieval system, except as may be expressly permitted by the 1976 Copyright Act or in writing from the publisher. Requests for permission should be addressed in writing to the following:

GlossaHouse, LLC 110 Callis Circle, Wilmore, KY 40309
www.GlossaHouse.com

Publisher's Cataloging-in-Publication Data

Leman, Marcus A.
    Reading with the Masoretes: The Exegetical Utility
    of Masoretic Accent Patterns

Marcus A. Leman— Wilmore, KY : GlossaHouse, ©2019.

xii, 176 pages ; 23 cm. -- (GlossaHouse Dissertation Series; volume 8) --

A revision of the author's doctoral dissertation from The Southern Baptist Theological Seminary 2017.

Library of Congress Control Number: 2019950119
ISBN: 9781942697893 (paperback)
ISBN: 9781942697909 (hardback)

The fonts used to create this work are available from linguistsoftware.com/lgku.htm.

Cover design by T. Michael W. Halcomb

Text layout by Marcus A. Leman in consultation with Fredrick J. Long

GLOSSAHOUSE DISSERTATION SERIES
GDS

The purpose and goal of the GlossaHouse Dissertation Series is to facilitate the creation and publication of innovative, affordable, and accessible scholarly resources—whether print or digital—that advance research in the areas of both ancient and modern texts and languages.

SERIES EDITORS

FREDRICK J. LONG ⬥ T. MICHAEL W. HALCOMB ⬥ CARL S. SWEATMAN

I dedicate this project to my wife, Rachel,
אשת חיל. In all things, my co-laborer.

Table of Contents

Abbreviations	xi
Preface	xii
Introduction	1
Chapter 1 Introduction	3
Chapter 2 Case Study: Etnachta after Direct Speech	33
Chapter 3 Case Study: Etnachta before *Ve'atah*	53

Chapter 4
    Case Study: Accents Framing
    Conditional Sentences
	79

Chapter 5 Case Study: Accents at Contrast Structures	113
Chapter 6 Conclusion	145
Appendix 1 Masoretic Accent Hierarchy	151
Appendix 2 Text Critical Work: Judges 16:13	155
Bibliography	159
Indices	169

Abbreviations

AD	*anno Domini*
ANE	Ancient Near East
BDB	Brown-Driver-Briggs Hebrew Lexicon
DS	Direct Speech
iDS	Indirect Speech
LXX	Septuagint
LXX-A	Septuagint text of Alexandrinus
LXX-B	Septuagint text of Vaticanus
MT	Masoretic Text
VSO	Verb-Subject-Object (word order)

Preface

When I began doctoral studies in the fall of 2013, I knew that I wanted to study two things: the Bible and the Hebrew language. When it came time to narrow in on a dissertation topic, I wanted one thing: to spend most of my time in the Hebrew text. This project embodies that desire in so many ways. Throughout the time of this study I listened to, read, studied, analyzed, and taught the book of Judges. I am still astounded by the covenant faithfulness of God towards a disobedient people in need of godly leadership. His grace was more than sufficient for his people of old, and his grace continues to abound to his people today (2 Cor 12:9).

Part of his grace comes to me through my amazing wife, Rachel. Her tireless partnership and sacrificial labor amazes me. She makes me a better man, encourages me to pursue my calling, and this work would not not exist without her contributions. Similarly, our children—Benaiah, Nathaniel, Greta, and Caleb—continue to teach me how to see God's wide world with fresh eyes. They inspire me to never stop learning.

I am thankful to Jason DeRouchie who helped me begin the journey of rigorous and faithful study of the Bible. His influence is seen throughout the textual layout in this project. Russell Fuller introduced me to the Masoretes like I had never known them before. His passion for the ancient reading tradition inspired me to take on this project. I am grateful for his steady guidance throughout the development of this dissertation. I am also blessed to have many friends who encouraged me, read articles, listened to my thoughts, and even reviewed my writing: Michael Graham, Kyle Bagwell, Richard McDonald, Adam Howell, Jesse Scheumann, and Scott McQuinn.

Throughout my studies, one verse has provided a constant reference point. Ezra 7:10 states that the good hand of God was upon him because "Ezra had set his heart to study the Law of the LORD, and to do it and to teach his statutes and rules in Israel." As a man desirous for God's hand on my life, I too strive to be a humble student, disciple, and teacher of God's word. May this dissertation constitute one small step on that journey and serve others in their pursuits.

Marcus A. Leman
Dallas, Texas
May 2019

Introduction

True genius and innovation often go unnoticed in their generation. History owns a fair number of Alexanders, Gutenbergs, and Wright brothers; those who see firsthand the immense impact of their deeds. Yet many stories of genius and innovation emerge as quiet ripples on the surface of a vast lake. The Masoretes offer one such story. Their tireless and quiet labors along the shores of Yam Kinneret ripple into the modern age.

While we know comparatively little about this ancient community of scribes and scholars, we still possess their genius. They believed that they had been entrusted with the ancient reading tradition passed down from Ezra himself. Yet this tradition was not written on the page, rather it was passed from generation to generation along with the sacred text. They took the incredible risk of writing this tradition in, around, above, and below the text so that it would be transmitted to future generations. Their efforts to preserve not just the substance of the text but also its "sense" were pure genius.

This project seeks to expose one layer of genius found in the Tiberian system of accentuating the Hebrew text of Scripture. The Masoretes accomplish numerous objectives with a singular system. One such accomplishment captures various syntactic realities of the text in accurate, consistent, and recognizable patterns. These accent patterns occur so consistently that the Masoretes can also use them to indicate semantic highlights by strategically breaking their pattern at key junctures. Yet even in breaking their patterns for the sake of other patterns or points of interest, they maintain a remarkable adherence to their principles.

This dissertation examines four major syntactic features and the Masoretic pattern for accenting them. Using the book of Judges as a contained corpus, each study presents the statistical occurrence of the pattern, clear examples of the pattern in action, and various types of divergence from the pattern. The chapter then examines each example of divergence for signs of intentionality. Clearly discernible reasons for divergence indicate the depth of the Masoretic insight into the text. Chapter 2 presents the pattern for Etnachta at the conclusion of mid-verse direct speech (e.g., Judg 1:3; 4:9; 6:20; 7:9–11; 8:20; 15:1). Chapter 3 examines the pattern for the interjection ועתה (*ve'atah*) from Genesis to Kings (e.g., Judg 13:7; 15:18; 1 Sam 9:13; 2 Kgs 7:9). Chapter 4 opens up the pattern for framing conditional clauses (e.g., Judg 4:8; 6:17; 9:15; 9:19–20; 11:30–31; 13:16; 13:23; 14:13; Gen 18:3; 28:20–22). Chapter 5 investigates the use of Masoretic accents in contexts of contrast, specifically in the presence of the contrast structures *vav* + X + verb, and *vav* + לא + verb (e.g., Judg 1:27; 2:17; 10:13).

Imagine sitting down to study the Hebrew Bible with a Masorete across the table. Who would not ask for comments in the midst of such a study session? The genius of the Masoretic accents illumine every page with their whispered comments. Those who learn to read with the accents, to hear what they have to say from ages past, learn to consult the ancient reading tradition. This is reading with the Masoretes.

CHAPTER 1

ARGUMENT AND BACKGROUND

1.1   THESIS

In recent decades, linguistic and literary methods of biblical interpretation have overshadowed reading the historical tradition written into the Hebrew text. While such methods offer new vantage points, they must be employed in conjunction with the historical tradition, not at its expense. The Masoretic *te'amim* (טעמים), commonly called "accents," serve three purposes in the text: (1) to signal the appropriate melody for chanting the text [cantillation]; (2) to mark the tone syllable of the word [accent]; (3) to parse the syntax of the verse [dichotomy].[1] All of these functions are important for conveying and receiving the "sense" (טעם) of the text. While students of biblical Hebrew typically learn a few accent names and rules, such a cursory introduction provides little towards understanding their exegetical utility. Reasons for the

---

[1]Joshua Jacobson, *Chanting the Hebrew Bible: The Art of Cantillation*, (Philadelphia: Jewish Publication Society, 2002), 13–14; Israel Yeivin, *Introduction to the Tiberian Masorah*, trans. E. J. Revell, MasS 5 (Missoula, MT: Scholars Press, 1980), 158; Geoffrey Khan, *A Short Introduction to the Tiberian Masoretic Bible and Its Reading Tradition,* ed. George Anton Kiraz (Piscataway, NJ: Gorgias, 2012), 37; William Wickes, "A Treatise on the Accentuation of the Three So-Called Poetical Books of the Old Testament, Psalms, Proverbs, and Job (טעמי אמ״ת)," in *Two Treatises on the Accentuation of the Old Testament,* ed. Harry M. Orlinsky (New York: KTAV, 1970), 2–3; Randall Buth, *Living Biblical Hebrew* ג: *Selected Readings with 500 Friends* (Jerusalem: Biblical Language Center, 2006), 115; James D. Price, *The Syntax of Masoretic Accents in the Hebrew Bible* (Lewiston, NY: Mellen, 1990), 11; Russell T. Fuller and Kyoungwon Choi, *Invitation to Biblical Hebrew Syntax: An Intermediate Grammar* (Grand Rapids: Kregel, 2016), 348–49.

neglect of the accent system in textbooks and classrooms range from active mistrust of the tradition to simple ignorance of its value. But the historic reading tradition has much to offer modern exegetes.

1.1.1 THESIS STATEMENT

Though interpreters commonly neglect the masoretic accents in exegesis, this system clarifies and confirms the sense of the text through highly predictable patterns.

1.1.2 THESIS EXPLANATION

Three components form the core of this thesis: (1) interpreters, (2) sense, and (3) patterns. "Interpreters" stands for anyone who reads the Hebrew text seeking to understand what it communicates. But, more specifically, it refers to those who do in-depth research and write interpretive commentary on the meaning of the text. The "neglect" of the accents often begins with a lack of training that leads to a subsequent lack of interest. Lode captures the experience of many:

> The vast majority of us were taught not to pay any attention to [the accents], or at most we have learned to recognize the middle of a verse by the accent Athnach, the upside-down v-shaped accent which occurs under the last word of the first half of the verse. Some of us have studied the Table of Accents inserted in our Biblia Hebraica, but few of us retain all their names, and rare are those who make constant use of the accents in their study and teaching—except for the rabbis.[2]

Price connects the lack of education to a lack of publication: "The study of the Masoretic accents in the Hebrew Old Testament has been

---

[2]Lars Lode, "A Discourse Perspective on the Significance of the Masoretic Accents," in Biblical Hebrew and Discourse Linguistics, ed. Robert D. Bergen (Dallas: Summer Institute of Linguistics, 1994), 155–174 at 155.

neglected by most Hebrew grammarians of this century. Most contemporary grammarians give only a brief description of the accents with a meager discussion of their function in the Hebrew Bible."[3] And Driver's testimony confirms that this trend has been going on for over a century: "[The accents] frequently offer material assistance in unravelling the sense of a difficult passage; and the best authorities continually appeal to them, on account of their bearing upon exegesis. Experience tells me how liable they are to be overlooked ... ."[4] While few interpreters explicitly demean the accents and set them aside as useless, the lack of use indicates the correctness of Driver's appraisal. Vain would be the search for a modern commentary that regularly and explicitly takes into account the accents.

The accent "system" encodes both the Masoretic reading tradition and their understanding of Hebrew grammar and syntax. The term *te'amim* literally means "sense." This sense refers to the groupings of words at the phrase and clause level, normally called syntax; it functions much like elaborate punctuation. But at times this sense refers to semantic highlights that function more like bold face, italics, or underline in order to attract the attention of the reader. The Masoretes have created an ingenious system that "confirms and clarifies" the sense of the text.[5] On one hand, the accents help to remove ambiguity that may exist in the reading (clarify), while on the other hand, they highlight the most important elements of the verse (confirm).

---

[3] James D. Price, The Syntax of Masoretic Accents in the Hebrew Bible (Lewiston, NY: Mellen, 1990), 5.

[4] Samuel R. Driver, A Treatise on the Use of the Tenses in Hebrew and Some Other Syntactical Questions (repr., Eugene, OR: Wipf and Stock, 2004), §88n1.

[5] While the Masoretes created the written symbols and system of accentuation, they did not create the tradition that it represents. The dissertation maintains this distinction throughout, though often referred to as Masoretic "choice."

This system operates according to orderly principles in conjunction with the grammar. Therefore, readers may consistently predict recurring "patterns." These accent patterns correspond to various syntactic features in the text. Such patterns benefit the exegete both in their regularity and occasional divergence from the pattern. The consistency of the Masoretic system provides a word-by-word commentary for anyone who learns to read their signs.

1.2 METHODOLOGY

The nature of this thesis requires an inductive, quantitative method of study in order to uncover patterns as they exist in the text. The presuppositions inherent to this dissertation lead to the following hypothesis—the Masoretes laid down the accents according to regular, discernible patterns based on syntactic and semantic considerations. This hypothesis requires the inductive definition of any such patterns in the text of Judges. After identifying apparent patterns in the text, this methodology systematically traces out the pattern through the entirety of the defined corpus. Each pattern will be investigated separately according to the demands of that pattern, for some are tied to words, others to clauses, and others to literary features. This stockpile of data leads to an analysis of whether or not this constitutes an "intentional pattern." Intentional patterns occur when they correspond with a grammatical-syntactical feature at a relatively high frequency (75 percent of the time).[6]

---

[6]The number 75 percent represents a general guideline, not an objective statistical threshold. All statistics throughout this dissertation represent "descriptive statistics" and no objective significance can be attributed to their values. Rather, the data is compiled and put it in statistical form so as to aid in discussion and further study. Achieving 75 percent triggers a deeper study of the "apparent pattern" looking

Discerning an intentional pattern requires analyzing more than just statistical recurrence. Intentionality manifests itself both in examples that conform to the pattern and those that diverge from the pattern. A divergence takes place when the conditions for the pattern in question (e.g., the mid-verse conclusion of direct speech) occur in a verse, but it does not receive the regular accent pattern. Any divergence from the intentional pattern reveals a conflict of Masoretic priorities in laying down the accents.[7] So, every divergence will be analyzed to discern why the Masoretes eschew their normal pattern. Generally speaking, these divergences come down to (1) a more significant pattern or syntactic feature supplanting the lesser pattern, or (2) the Masoretes offering semantic insight. Each individual study constitutes a success when an intentional pattern emerges with purposeful divergence. The numerous examples found in these studies illustrate both the accent patterns and their usefulness for exegesis.

Four potential patterns form the backbone of this dissertation. For these case studies a general outline defines each chapter in order to provide continuity:

---

for an "intentional pattern." For more on statistics in corpus related research, see Tony McEnery and Andrew Hardie, *Corpus Linguistics: Method, Theory and Practice* (New York: Cambridge, 2012), 48–53.

[7] One might object at this point that the Masoretes were merely recording their tradition, almost in a mindless or slavish manner. The intention here is not to depict the Masoretes as innovators of a new tradition; they clearly intended to pass along that which they had received. The intent behind calling these "Masoretic priorities" and "Masoretic patterns" simply indicates that the Masoretes were intelligent scribes of the tradition that comes to us by their hands. The tradition they recorded contained a highly complex system of ranked disjunctions which occur according to regular patterns and principles. This dissertation labels them "Masoretic" because they come to us through the pen of the Masoretes though they long predated the Tiberian community.

1. Grammatical Considerations—Each case study demands clear definitions on grammatical terms involved in the examination. This section will detail terms and grammatical categories used throughout the study.

2. Summary of Research Data—This section contains statistics from the quantitative study and charts of every individual example. This compact presentation of data will serve as a reference point for the entire chapter.

3. Outline of the Masoretic Pattern—Utilizing the clearest examples, this unit presents the Masoretic accent pattern that arises from the data. Each example will include the full Hebrew text with running commentary (no translation will be provided).

4. Divergence From the Pattern—Perhaps the most important section of each chapter, this unit presents the most difficult divergences from the Masoretic pattern. These divergences will appear categorically according to the perceived basis for each divergence, thus reducing the number of full examples presented in the text.

Within this general outline, the demands of each study define the sub-categories of the discussion. For example, the grammatical discussion for contrast structures may extend further than in the case study on conditionals, since contrast structures require more definition. Or, the summary of research data in the case study on *ve'atah* may extend broader than in the study on direct speech, since *ve'atah* only occurs a handful of times in the book of Judges. But this general outline will provide consistency across chapters and allow for ease of reading.

1.3   THREE-FOLD FUNCTION OF ACCENTS

One foundational assumption of this study relates to the three-fold function of the accents. Scholars universally recognize three functions of the accent system which all play a part in conveying the sense of the text.[8] The accents function first to mark word stress. Generally speaking, the accent falls on the stressed syllable of the word; hence the name, "accent." Some accents come only before or after the word,[9] but occasionally the Masoretes marked such accents twice—once in the proper position and once on the stressed syllable.[10] This function of the accents provides minor exegetical assistance in disambiguating identical verbal forms (e.g., Gen 29:6, 9; 1 Kgs 8:48).

The accents function secondly to indicate the melody to be sung on each word. Contrary to modern, Western music notation, each symbol stands for a musical trope—a unique melodic pattern—rather than one individual note. Binder notes that, "The style of Biblical chant is half-musical and half-declamatory, the reader always being mindful of the meaning of the text and welding it to the tropes."[11] Joshua Jacobson comments that, "The *te'amim* serve to flesh out the bare bones of the scriptural text with an element of expressivity."[12] In other words, as the musical tropes bind themselves to the text, the meaning of a word or phrase takes on a more lifelike expression. Though the musical expression has changed throughout history and in various geographic locations, it conveys the sense of the text when read aloud.[13] This

---

[8]Though these functions are "universally" recognized, scholars debate the priority of each function in the history of the tradition.

[9]Pre-positive accents include Yetiv, Telisha Gedolah; post-positive accents include Segol, Pashta, Zarqa, Telisha Qetanah.

[10]The Masoretes only double the accent Pashta when it occurs *mil'el*. The Koren Bible provides all occurrences of these pre- and post-positive accents in duplicate form so that they mark word stress while maintaining their traditional position.

[11]Abraham W. Binder, *Biblical Chant* (New York: Sacred Music Press, 1959), 15.

[12]Jacobson, *Chanting the Hebrew Bible: The Art of Cantillation*, 9.

[13]Numerous modern interpretations of the tropes exist within these general geographic groupings: Ashkenazic, Sephardic, Moroccan, Egyptian, Syrian,

second function of the accents is commonly called "cantillation" or "chanting."

The accents function thirdly to convey the sense of the text by marking the hierarchical, syntactical breaks of the verse.[14] This function resembles a rather elaborate form of punctuation.[15] Yet, this is far more than mere punctuation. Price writes, "The accents complement the grammar and syntax of Hebrew, preserving the traditional understanding of the text, an understanding with roots in the deep recesses of antiquity. No serious expositor of Scripture should neglect

---

Baghdadian, and Yemenite. Each cantillation system exhibits elements of its own historical and geographic development. Yet, the similarities between these systems point to a common Palestinian origin (Binder, *Biblical Chant*, 14).

[14] Elan Dresher has published one notable exception to this claim. He argues that the accents do not mark the syntax of a verse but rather the prosody, or reading rhythm. While he acknowledges that syntax and prosody share a huge common domain, he maintains that examples exist where the author is clearly marking prosody and not syntax (see Bezalel Elan Dresher, "The Prosodic Basis of the Tiberian System of Hebrew Accents," *Language* 70 [March 1994]: 1–52; Bezalel Elan Dresher, "Biblical Accents: Prosody" in *Encyclopedia of Hebrew Language and Linguistics* [Boston: Brill, 2013], 288–96). Two considerations must be raised against this assertion. First, the musical dimension of the accents often plays a dominant role in determining the precise accent used in a given phrase. The ancients would rarely read a text silently, and when read aloud they would often chant the words to a melody (Jacobson, *Chanting the Hebrew Bible: The Art of Cantillation*, 173). Thus, reciting a text aloud was not the same as everyday speech. See also Norman Janis, "A Grammar of the Biblical Accents" (PhD diss., Harvard University, 1987), 59. In other words, if the accents primarily mark prosody, is it a prosody of the chant or of the spoken Hebrew language? This is very difficult to determine. Second, there exists a clear hierarchy in the accent system. While every accent exhibits conjunctive or disjunctive features, within the disjunctive category each accent holds a rank relative to the others. Stronger accents (e.g., Etnachta, Zaqef) control greater portions of the text and offer a more pronounced syntactical break (William Wickes, "A Treatise on the Accentuation of the Twenty-One So-Called Prose Books of the Old Testament [טעמי כ"א ספרים]," in *Two Treatises on the Accentuation of the Old Testament,* ed. Harry M. Orlinsky [New York: KTAV, 1970], 29).

[15] Jacobson, *Chanting the Hebrew Bible: The Art of Cantillation*, 23.

such important keys to Biblical exposition."[16] The Masoretes signify the syntax of a verse according to three considerations: syntactic, clausal, and semantic.[17] The conjunctive or disjunctive nature of the accents group words into individual clauses (syntactic use). The hierarchy of the accents builds relationships between these individual clauses (clausal use).[18] And occasionally the Masoretes chose to use the strongest accents to mark special points of interest (semantic use). These three syntactical functions help to clarify and confirm the sense of the text.

1.4   MASORETIC RIGOR AND FIDELITY

A second presupposition influences the direction of this dissertation: the Masoretes faithfully passed on the tradition that they received. Though scholars debate the origin of the term "Masorete" (בעל מסרה), these men clearly sought to "pass along their tradition" (מסר). While they innovated a means of writing down Hebrew vowels and syntactic markers, they preserved the historic reading tradition that was passed down to them.[19] They display their diligence in the precise pointings (נקודות), flowing accents (טעמים), and marginal commentary (מסורה). Historically, scholars have recognized the rigorous and faithful work that these men passed on to later generations. This dissertation does not

---

[16]Price, *Syntax of Masoretic Accents*, 9.

[17]Fuller and Choi, *Biblical Hebrew Syntax*, Accents §9.

[18]While the term "clause" takes various definitions, it minimally refers to a unit that contains a subject and predicate. This dissertation will consistently use the term clause to refer to such units, whereas "phrase" will be used more generally for units without a finite verb.

[19]For a lengthy discussion of this issue, see Dominique Barthélemy, *Studies in the Text of the Old Testament: An Introduction to the Hebrew Old Testament Text Project*, trans. Sarah Lind, vol. 3 of *Textual Criticism and the Translator* (Winona Lake, IN: Eisenbrauns, 2012), 13.

overtly explore the question of whether or not the Masoretes always got the Hebrew "right;" rather, it presents the reading tradition they passed on in the accents and the reader may determine if this makes the best sense of the grammar and syntax.

The work of the Masoretes meets the written page in medieval times, not in antiquity. Thus, documenting the transmission of their work represents a very different challenge than tracing the transmission of the ancient Hebrew text. The Aleppo Codex contains the very markings of a chief Masorete and constitutes an original document.[20] Scholars reconstruct the missing portions of Aleppo from other key documents, most importantly from the Leningrad Codex, purported to have been copied from Aleppo.[21] Thus, access to these original manuscripts, or near original, greatly simplifies the examination of the Masoretic marks and notations.

The Masoretes serve as faithful guides to reading the Hebrew text. Further, we possess the core of their tradition straight from the hands of ben-Asher. While the reader does not need to share these convictions in order to benefit from this study, one must understand such presuppositions in order to make sense of the analysis. Due to the inductive nature of this study, the results offer benefits to anyone seeking to better read and understand biblical Hebrew as found in the Masoretic text. This study seeks to uncover patterns in the Masoretic accents that will provide historical, exegetical confirmation that the

---

[20]Most of Torah portion of the Aleppo Codex was lost during a 1947 riot in Aleppo, Syria. These lost portions are presumed to have been burned or torn out of the codex. The text begins in Deut 28 and ends in Song 5, with various portions of the prophets missing, as well as Esther, Ezra-Nehemiah, and Chronicles.

[21]Yosef Ofer, "The History and Authority of the Aleppo Codex," in *Jerusalem Crown: Companion Volume,* ed. Mordechai Glatzer (Jerusalem: N. Ben-Zvi Printing Enterprises, 2002), 25–50 at 36.

modern reader has understood the text correctly. In other words, a truly historical-grammatical hermeneutic will refer to the *historical* tradition of the Masoretes in the accent system to clarify and confirm a *grammatical* reading of the text.

1.5   HISTORICAL BACKGROUND

Aharon ben-Asher, the great Masorete of the Aleppo Codex, points back to Ezra and his contemporaries as the initiators of the Masoretic tradition.[22] Israel Yeivin summarizes the historical progression:

> It appears that the first to work on Masoretic matters were the *soferim*—the pupils of Ezra the Scribe in the early second temple period. Their work extended into the period of the Talmud (300–600 CE). After this the period of the Masoretes began, and their work continued until the final establishment of the received Tiberian tradition, including its vocalization and accentuation, in the tenth century. To some extent the work of clarifying the textual tradition, and preserving it according to the tradition of the Masorah, has continued up to our time.[23]

Trained men faithfully passed down the reading tradition for many centuries until it was recorded over the consonantal text. Even after scribes began writing out the reading tradition, they contiued to orally pass down both the vowels and accents.[24] Thus, trained men passed down the proper reading of the text from Ezra's time, nearly 1400 years, until ben-Asher inscribed it in the consummate Tiberian codex, the Crown of Aleppo.

Not only were the Masoretes well trained as scribes, they lived in a vibrant Hebrew-speaking community. Though their Hebrew

---

[22] Fuller and Choi, *Biblical Hebrew Syntax*, Accents §1.
[23] Yeivin, *Introduction to the Tiberian Masorah*, 131–32.
[24] Jacobson, *Chanting the Hebrew Bible: The Art of Cantillation*, 363.

undoubtedly differed from that of David or Moses, their continued use of the language alongside scholarly endeavors infuses the tradition with a living quality. Kutscher writes,

> There is reason to believe that at the beginning of the present millennium Hebrew was employed to a certain extent as the language of instruction in Jewish schools in the Moslem countries.... *In tenth-century Palestine we hear about Hebrew being spoken in Tiberias*; in Jerusalem in the fifteenth century, even non-Jewish travelers report this fact.... In Yemen until very recently the Rabbi's sermon was delivered in Hebrew. Talmud and Mishnah were taught in Hebrew and scholars sometimes conversed with one another in Hebrew.[25]

This use of Hebrew in Tiberias, home of the ben-Asher family, provides a deeper understanding of how these men related to Hebrew on a daily basis. Ofer gives more details about the use of Hebrew in Tiberias,

> In the tenth century a Hebrew grammarian of the city wrote a work that has been preserved in part in the Cairo Genizah. He relates that he studied the accent of the people of Tiberias, especially their way of pronouncing the letter *resh* when reading the Bible and when speaking Hebrew. To that end he would spend long hours in the city streets and squares, listening to the speech of ordinary people, in Hebrew and in Aramaic. This description, which is written in Arabic, indicates that in the tenth century Hebrew was actually spoken in Tiberias and was not only a literary or liturgical language.[26]

Thus, the accent system written into the text during the tenth century came from trained scribes who used Hebrew on a daily basis in their homes and markets. This level of fluency with the Hebrew language only bolsters the credibility of their work.

While multiple systems of vocalization and accentuation existed, the tradition of the Tiberian Masoretes developed the greatest

---

[25]Eduard Yechezkel Kutscher, *A History of the Hebrew Language* (Leiden: Brill, 1982), 149.

[26]Yosef Ofer, "History and Authority," 50.

precision.[27] The Tiberian tradition began between AD 600–800 and climaxed with the work of Aharon ben-Asher in AD 915.[28] The Tiberian system builds on the consonantal text via three elements: (1) symbols for the vowels above and below the text along with other diacritical marks; (2) symbols commonly called accents to mark word stress, musical trope, and syntax; and (3) the Masoretic notes to ensure accurate transmission of the text. While consonantal scrolls remain a cornerstone of Jewish synagogue worship, Masoretic codices became the pedagogical, scribal, and liturgical touchstone.[29]

1.6 HISTORY OF RESEARCH

While it may seem anachronistic to examine evidence preceding the time of the Masoretes, the same syntactical groupings that the Masoretes encoded had been read and reflected upon for centuries. Thus, while no ancient author laid out explicit syntactic principles prior to the Masoretes, translators were reading the Hebrew and making decisions about how to represent it in another language.[30] Their *use* of the Hebrew can provide insights into how the ancients were reading the text before

---

[27] This dissertation will deal with only the accent system of the Tiberian Masoretes. While the principles herein may apply to the other systems of notation, this study has been conducted entirely in the Tiberian system. Yosef Ofer, an expert on the Aleppo Codex, writes, "Other systems of vocalization—the Babylonian and Palestinian systems—are known to us, but the tradition preserved by the Masoretes of Tiberias is acknowledged as the most advanced and the most precise" (Ofer, "History and Authority," 27). Revell adds, "[The] Palestinian MSS are distinguished from other MSS representing the Western tradition by their writing system only, not by the reading tradition which it represented" (*Biblical Texts with Palestinian Pointing and Their Accents* [Missoula, MT: Scholars Press, 1977], 185).

[28] Wickes, "Accentuation of the Twenty-One Prose Books," 7; Yeivin, *Introduction to the Tiberian Masorah*, 12.

[29] Jacobson, *Chanting the Hebrew Bible: The Art of Cantillation*, 13.

[30] Yeivin, *Introduction to the Tiberian Masorah*, 218.

the Masoretic tradition was encoded. This paradigm exhibits itself most clearly in the word-for-word translation portions of the Septuagint, Targums, and even the Vulgate.[31] Every translation must make interpretive decisions from time to time. Both interpretive translation and the straight-forward rendering of passages may offer insight into what the Masoretes do with the accents. In other words, scholars often check ancient translations to see how they understood the Hebrew language. Such a process may also be used with profit to see how translators understood the Hebrew reading tradition in centuries prior to the Masoretes.

1.6.1 Early Accent Studies

In the introduction to the 1970 KTAV reprint of William Wickes's two treatises on the accent system, Aron Dotan provides an extensive survey of the major contributions to Masoretic accent research.[32] His survey covers the most significant figures and their writings from the time of Aharon ben-Asher and the Masoretes down to the time of the KTAV reprint of Wickes. Without reproducing Dotan's discussion of these works, this study draws out some highlights that relate specifically to using the accents for exegesis and then proceeds to mention more recent publications since the reprint of Wickes.

Appropriately Dotan begins with Aharon ben-Asher, the Masorete credited with putting down the vocalization and accentuation of the famed Aleppo Codex.[33] This early treatise, ספר דקדוקי הטעמים,

---

[31]The Syriac Peshitta may also provide some assistance, especially where the Targums are more expansive and interpretive. Other translations may prove useful, but these comprise the three or four essential translations that assist with this process.
[32]See also Yeivin, *Introduction to the Tiberian Masorah*, §181–91.
[33]Ofer, "History and Authority," 27.

CHAPTER 1: ARGUMENT AND BACKGROUND 17

gives birth to the new discipline of Masoretic studies as ben-Asher defines basic rules of accentuation.[34] Dotan then mentions a few other Arabic and Hebrew treatises from that early time period which accomplish objectives similar to that of ben-Asher (i.e., providing rules for accentuation and other aspects of masorah). These early treatises expound upon an innovation in the textual history among people who possessed a living, oral tradition. It was not until centuries later that those far removed from the original Masoretic community would begin to study and write. For later scholars the tradition came primarily through these written accents.

Half a millennium after ben-Asher, Elijah Levita rekindled the study of accents and fanned the flame among Christian scholars of the West.[35] During this time Samuel Bohlius recorded a classification of the disjunctive accents into four strata based on divisional strength.[36] Caspar Ledebuhr and Matthias Wasmuth built on this class division but made only minor innovations. The Masoretes intend for readers to recognize and reflect the relative weight of pauses in the reading. This concept of accent hierarchy is not only important for musical reading of the text but also for proper exegesis. Stronger divisions effectively incorporate all weaker divisions within their domain. Thus, this hierarchy of accent classes becomes an important key to reading the accents rightly.

This initial Christian research not only influenced other Christian scholars but their Jewish counterparts as well. One of the most prominent Jewish scholars on the accents was Shlomo Hanau who wrote

---

[34]Wickes, "Accentuation of the Three Poetical Books," viii–ix.

[35]Wickes, "Accentuation of the Three Poetical Books," viii. Levita's commentary on the Masorah finds a response in Johannes Buxtorf's *Tiberias* published in 1620. This interchange sparked a multigenerational debate on the origination of the vowels and accents (Barthélemy, *Studies in the Text of the Old Testament*, 13).

[36]Wickes, "Accentuation of the Three Poetical Books," x.

שערי זמרה.[37] He too embraced the classification scheme and began to explore the relationship between syntax structure and accent patterns.[38] Seligman Baer includes a chapter in his תורת אמת on how to accent a text.[39] Such punctuation proficiency provides the reader with valuable insight into alternative accentuations of a verse. This knowledge greatly aids the exegetical process by virtue of contrasting possibilities. Another nineteenth-century author, grammarian Samuel David Luzzatto, records his interpretation on a host of verses based on the Masoretic accentuation. Many of these verses and difficulties were not new to the literature, but Dotan considers his compilation of references and commentary to be quite useful.[40]

1.6.2   The Influence of William Wickes

All streams of Masoretic accent study in the English language necessarily reference the fountain of William Wickes's two treatises. His original study and presentation of the accents has achieved a classic status on par with Gesenius's Hebrew grammar. But Wickes does not just provide the English language with a benchmark study, he also makes significant advancements in this field. Dotan details these advancements: (1) his synthesis of nineteenth-century Jewish scholars and seventeenth-century Christian scholars, (2) his adoption and application of the principle of continuous dichotomy, and (3) the scientific elaboration of the rules of accentuation.[41] Dotan also points to the clearest defect of the work, Wickes's (mis-)use of manuscript

---

[37]Shlomo Hanau, שערי זמרה הארוך (Brooklyn: Rabbi Y. A. Guttman, 2003).
[38]Wickes, "Accentuation of the Three Poetical Books," xii.
[39]Wickes, "Accentuation of the Three Poetical Books," xv.
[40]Wickes, "Accentuation of the Three Poetical Books," xv.
[41]Wickes, "Accentuation of the Three Poetical Books," xvi.

material and his willingness to emend the text.[42] But the value of these treatises far outweighs their flaws. Wickes's work overflows with clearly stated principles and examples. He believed that a thorough understanding of the accents would aid in exegesis, not distract from it.[43] He helps readers come to this conclusion by establishing the logical, syntactic, and semantic deployment of the accents. He writes of semantic use of the accents, "In their desire to mark emphasis, [the Masoretes] did not scruple to pass over the most prominent logical pauses. (These pauses were indeed marked by musical pauses, but *the main musical pause* was reserved for the emphasis)."[44] This distinction proves fundamental to exegesis.

1.6.3   POST-WICKES: DEVELOPMENTS

The next full treatment of the accents to be offered comes from Arthur Spanier in *Die Massoretischen Akzente.* His book (1) examines common accent combinations, (2) analyzes phrase and sentence structure, and (3) provides a study of the Babylonian system of accents in order to compare with the Tiberian system. Dotan calls this an "internal historical study of the accentuation system itself."[45] Spanier concludes that the accents primarily serve a rhetorical purpose over the their musical and exegetical roles.[46] Yet, Spanier also concludes that the accents represent the tradition received by the Masoretes in antiquity.[47]

---

[42]Wickes, "Accentuation of the Three Poetical Books," xix, xxiii.
[43]Wickes, "Accentuation of the Three Poetical Books," 5.
[44]Wickes, "Accentuation of the Twenty-One Prose Books," 33.
[45]Wickes, "Accentuation of the Three Poetical Books," xxxiv.
[46]Wickes, "Accentuation of the Three Poetical Books," xxxvi.
[47]Arthur Spanier, *Die Massoretischen Akzente—Eine Darlegung Ihres Systems Nebst Beiträgen zum Verständnis Ihrer Entwicklung* (Berlin: Akademie-Verlag, 1927), 112.

Their fidelity to the tradition gives the modern exegete more confidence that he is in fact reading with the ancients.

In the conclusion of his book, פיסוק טעמים שבמקרא, Mordecai Breuer devotes twenty-five pages to interpretation of the accents.[48] He catalogs example after example of verses which could be read multiple ways. After presenting various historic and rabbinic interpretations he parses the Masoretic accents to reveal their interpretation. He emphasizes in that chapter how the accents bring clarity to an otherwise ambiguous verse. He writes,

טעמי המקרא הם אוצר בלום של פרשנות, פיסוק וקריאה נאה ומתוקנת. הרוצה לעמוד על פשוטו של מקרא, ימצא בהם את מיטב הפירושים, המסורים, ומקובלים לכתבי הקודש.[49]

Thus, the accents are not only the key to understanding the Masoretic reading tradition, they offer the best understanding of the text itself (מיטב הפירושים). Breuer then seeks to prove this point by showing how the Masoretes skillfully render the clearest understanding of the text via the accents.

Moshe H. Goshen-Gottstein contributes to the stream of research on the accent system tangentially through his writings on the Aleppo Codex. He has been a chief advocate of the position that Aleppo resides in the earliest stratum of Masoretic codices;[50] with this codex as the

---

[48]Mordecai Breuer was also a foundational figure in producing כתר ירושלים, a Hebrew Bible based on the text and graphical formatting of the Aleppo Codex.

[49]Mordecai Breuer, פיסוק טעמים שבמקרא: תורת דקדוק הטעמים, (Jerusalem: World Zionist Organization [ההסתדרות הציונית], 1958), 135. Breuer's quote in translation, "The *te'amim* of the reading, they are a treasure packed full of interpretation, punctuation, and a fitting and proper reading. The one desiring to stand upon the literalness of the reading, he will find in them the best interpretations, dedicated and acceptable to the sacred writings."

[50]Moshe H. Goshen-Gottstein, "The Rise of the Tiberian Bible Text," in *Biblical and Other Studies,* ed. Alexander Altmann (Cambridge: Harvard University Press, 1963), 79–122 at 85. See also Moshe H. Goshen-Gottstein, "The Aleppo Codex

original Masoretic document *par excellence*.⁵¹ These conclusions may appear to many as aloof from the ground-level work of exegesis in this thesis. Yet, to have an original Masoretic document from which to work is phenomenally significant, for we need not debate which accents the Masoretes actually penned—we have them. Goshen-Gottstein goes on to emphasize the Masoretic motivation:

> The Masoretes were convinced, rightly in their way, that they were keeping up an ancient tradition, and interfering with it purposely would have been for them the worst crime possible. Yet they were extremely proud, quite justifiably, of their own achievement: the graphic notation and its perfection, so as to safeguard the ancient tradition for all future generations.⁵²

These men understood that their reading tradition came orally from Ezra, through the scribes, and they had managed to encode it for faithful future reading.⁵³ While accepting such claims requires trusting historical testimony, evidence also continues to confirm the ancient character of the Masoretic tradition.⁵⁴

Miles B. Cohen understands Wickes and Breuer to have recorded the best summary of all prior accent study up to the time of writing his book *The System of Accentuation in the Hebrew Bible*.⁵⁵ His work is largely a condensation and generalization of these two

---

and the Rise of the Massoretic Bible Text," *The Biblical Archaeologist* 42 (Summer 1979): 145–63.

⁵¹Moshe H. Goshen-Gottstein, "The Authenticity of the Aleppo Codex," in *Text and Language in Bible and Qumran* (Jerusalem: Orient, 1960), 17–58 at 58.

⁵²Goshen-Gottstein, "The Rise of the Tiberian Bible Text," 96.

⁵³Yeivin, *Introduction to the Tiberian Masorah*, 131–32; Ofer, "History and Authority," 32; Khan, *A Short Introduction*, 61; Fuller and Choi, *Biblical Hebrew Syntax*, Accents §1.

⁵⁴See Michael Segal et al., "An Early Leviticus Scroll From En-Gedi: Preliminary Publication," *Textus* 26 (2016): 1–30.

⁵⁵Miles B. Cohen, *The System of Accentuation in the Hebrew Bible* (Minneapolis: Milco Press, 1969), 10.

systematic presentations of the accents. He summarizes, "The טעמים ... do not represent any fixed punctuation marks, corresponding to commas or semi-colons, for instance, but rather denote only relative degrees of pause, dependent on disjunctive level and sentence position."[56] In order to help present these relative relationships, Cohen provides numerous examples of bracketed verses similar to Breuer. Learning to bracket verses in this manner may help those still learning the accents to quickly visualize the text divisions and aid in exegesis.

Aron Dotan has himself contributed a number of publications that are significant to the study of the accent system. But Dotan's purview of study generally takes in the whole breadth of the Masoretic system, and he is known more for his works related to masorah. Still, his reprint of Aharon Ben-Asher's דקדוקי הטעמים stands at the top of the list.[57] He has also provided readers with an accurate printed copy of the Leningrad Codex in his *Biblia Hebraica Leningradensia*.[58] Rather than focusing on text critical issues, as in the *Stuttgartensia*, Dotan's *Leningradensia* focuses on reproduction of an extant traditional text. But his work extends far beyond reproduction of historic Masoretic texts and treatises. He has authored the thoroughgoing article "Masorah" in *Encyclopedia Judaica*.[59] While this article gives a far more truncated explanation of the accents than a monograph like

---

[56] Cohen, *System of Accentuation in the Hebrew Bible*, 37.

[57] Aharon Ben-Asher, *The Diqduqe Hate'amim of Aharon Ben Moshe Ben Asher: With a Critical Edition of the Original Text from New Manuscripts,* ed. Aron Dotan (Jerusalem: Academy of the Hebrew Language, 1967).

[58] *Biblia Hebraica Leningradensia: Prepared According to the Vocalization, Accents, and Masora of Aaron Ben Moses Ben Asher in the Leningrad Codex,* ed. Aron Dotan (Peabody, MA: Henrickson, 2001).

[59] Aron Dotan, "Masorah," in vol. 13 of *Encyclopedia Judaica* (New York: Macmillan Reference, 2007), 603–56.

Wickes, the brevity is actually a strength. It serves as a good starting point for those seeking to understand the accent system and its relationship to the entire Masoretic tradition. Another focal point of this article, and one previously published, is the relative chronology of the Hebrew vowels points and accents.[60] He posits that the accent symbols actually pre-date the vocalization symbols because readers were far more likely to struggle with proper cantillation and punctuation than with pronunciation.[61] These writings, and many others, have made him a leader in the field of Masoretic studies.

Israel Yeivin's *Introduction to the Tiberian Masorah* stands out as a concise and clear guide among modern contributors.[62] After a brief discussion of major manuscripts (Part 1), Yeivin provides an overview of the Masorah (Part 2) and then details the nature and behavior of the accent system (Part 3). His presentation focuses far more on the accents of the twenty-one books (כ"א) than for those of the three books (אמ"ת). In addition to his own brief history of research on the accents, Yeivin spends most of his time presenting the function of the accents according to a hierarchic system.[63] On interpretation of the accents he writes:

> Commentators—and also the versions—generally understand the text in a way consistent with the accents. Commentators sometimes refer to the accentuation of a verse, and only rarely do they explain the text in a way which conflicts with the accentuation.... In his Sefer Moznayim Ibn Ezra says 'You should not listen to, or agree with, any interpretation which is not consistent with the accentuation'.[64]

---

[60] Aron Dotan, "The Relative Chronology of Hebrew Vocalization and Accentuation," *Proceedings of the American Academy for Jewish Research* 48 (1981): 87–99.

[61] Dotan, "Masorah," 627.

[62] Yeivin, *Introduction to the Tiberian Masorah*.

[63] Yeivin, *Introduction to the Tiberian Masorah*, 176–218.

[64] Yeivin, *Introduction to the Tiberian Masorah*, 218.

Readers should note the clarity of Yeivin's introductory work which provides a gateway into understanding the accent system within the context of the full Masoretic tradition.

E. J. Revell, who translated Yeivin into English, should also be recognized for his own works related to the accent system: *Nesiga (Retraction of Word Stress) in Tiberian Hebrew*, and *The Pausal System: Divisions in the Hebrew Biblical Text as Marked by Voweling and Stress Position*.[65] As far as using the accents for exegesis, Revell's *Nesiga* study provides little except to call into question the phonemic nature of Hebrew, and whether or not the accent stress markings actually indicate this principle. But Revell's study of the pausal system exhibits significant influence on the exegetical discussion. He summarizes the pattern of pausals: "Pausal forms mark the ends of clauses, or of 'sentences', i.e., semantic units formed by two or more clauses. Rarely they occur within clauses, again marking a division made on a semantic unit."[66] Revell concludes that the pausal system represents a different system of text division than what the accents represent. In his opinion, the fact that the Masoretes faithfully represent both systems, despite their occasional clashes, attests to the "antiquity and reliability" of their work.[67] Such factors may influence some of the examples provided throughout this dissertation, but this study remains focused on the

---

[65]E. J. Revell, *Nesiga (Retraction of Word Stress) in Tiberian Hebrew* (Madrid: Instituto de Filologia, C.S.I.C., 1987); E. J. Revell, *The Pausal System: Divisions in the Hebrew Biblical Text as Marked by Voweling and Stress Position,* ed. Raymond de Hoop and Paul Sanders (Sheffield: Sheffield Phoenix, 2015). Revell has also published *Biblical Texts with Palestinian Pointing and their Accents* (Missoula, MT: Scholars Press, 1977).

[66]E. J. Revell, "Pausal Forms in Biblical Hebrew: Their Function, Origin, and Significance," *JSS* 25 (1980): 165–79 at 167–68.

[67]Revell, "Pausal Forms in Biblical Hebrew," 177.

patterns of the accent system and their utility in exegesis of the text.[68]

James Price has contributed a full monograph entitled *The Syntax of Masoretic Accents in the Hebrew Bible*.[69] With the assistance of computer testing and tabulation, Price seeks to delineate the syntactical structure and rules of the accent system as thoroughly as possible. While he generally holds Wickes in high esteem, Price does not hesitate to take issue with certain principles, especially the "law of continuous dichotomy."[70] He also presents the accents in terms of hierarchic relationships, similar to Yeivin, which again differs slightly from Wickes.[71] Price not only discusses the rules of accentuation, he also seeks to guide his readers into proper interpretation of the accents according to their hierarchies and syntax. His most important contribution has been to categorize accents of the same class into "near" and "remote" subordinates of their master accent.[72] In any given domain, the ruling accent will possess a near and far subordinate. If only one occurs it will be the near subordinate; but when both occur, the far

---

[68] Revell writes that it is not possible to determine which system of pause, vocalic or accentual, was instituted first ("Pausal Forms in Biblical Hebrew," 169). While this study gives some attention to the relationship of these two systems, it will not speculate as to which is more original. Revell's conclusion that these represent two independent systems, while not supported here, does not constitute sufficient cause to doubt the value of the accent patterns for exegesis.

[69] Price has also published *Concordance of the Hebrew Accents in the Hebrew Bible*, 5 vols. (Lewiston, NY: Mellen, 1996).

[70] Price, *Syntax of Masoretic Accents*, 40–44, 171–85.

[71] Wickes, "Accentuation of the Three Poetical Books," 11. Wickes rejects using terms of medieval nobility to describe hierarchy, but he does not provide a succinct hierarchical gradation—he prefers only "pausal" and "non-pausal," making some allowance for the term *servi*. His principles on hierarchy must be discerned from his overall presentation of first, second, and third level breaks in a given verse.

[72] See this more fully developed in Fuller and Choi, *Biblical Hebrew Syntax*, Accents §2.C.

subordinate exercises more authority than its counterpart subordinate.[73] This volume, and especially this last principle, constitutes a useful reference tool alongside Wickes and Yeivin for clarifying rules of accentuation.

Geoffrey Khan's book *A Short Introduction to the Tiberian Masoretic Bible and Its Reading Tradition* touches on eight basic elements: (1) consonantal text, (2) layout of the text, (3) paragraphs, (4) accents, (5) vocalization, (6) notes, (7) treatises, (8) oral tradition. In addition to this he provides a discussion of Tiberian pronunciation and a list of resources for each of the eight components of the Masoretic reading tradition. He understands the accents, and the chant they signify, to mark "the semantic and syntactic connections between words and phrases."[74] This function of the accents can be traced back to the Babylonian Talmud prior to their inscription by the Masoretes.[75] Thus, Khan provides readers with a basic overview of the function of the accents in the context of the greater Masoretic tradition, but this particular work offers little direction for determining their exegetical utility.[76]

Rachel Mashiah has produced some articles in English related to her unpublished dissertation on parallel accent patterns, which was

---

[73]Price, *Syntax of Masoretic Accents*, 25–26. See ch. 4 of this dissertation for more details on this approach to hierarchy among the accents.

[74]Khan, *Short Introduction*, 37.

[75]Khan, *Short Introduction*, 38.

[76]Khan has also been instrumental in editing the *Encyclopedia of Hebrew Language and Linguistics* (Boston: Brill, 2013). Numerous articles in these volumes are relevant to the study of the Masoretic accents (e.g., "Prosody" [Dresher], "Tiberian Reading Tradition" [Khan]). Khan has also written multiple volumes on the Karaite tradition which bears numerous connections to the Masoretic tradition, though this does not often provide much insight on the Masoretic accents. See Geoffrey Khan, *The Early Karaite Tradition of Hebrew Grammatical Thought* (Boston: Brill, 2000).

supervised by Aron Dotan.⁷⁷ She defines a parallel patterns as "accentual segments identical in their divisional structure and terminating disjunctive, yet differing in their accentuation."⁷⁸ The study seeks to describe actual usage of the accents in order to determine prescriptive principles for accentuation. She observes "that there is a tendency to accentuate those verses that have a certain characteristic in common similarly, yet no valid rules could be deduced on the basis of this tendency."⁷⁹ In other words, when we see verses sharing a syntactic pattern, we could justifiably expect to see similar accentuation. Whereas her study focuses on *the pattern of an entire chains of accents*, this dissertation looks mainly at the terminal disjunctives of grammatical patterns in order to determine what textual features the Masoretes sought to prioritize via their accentuation.

1.6.1 Post Wickes. Objections

Norman Janis presents a dissertation exploring the ways in which the accents record the speech pattern of the Masoretic reading tradition. He writes:

> The apparently disparate functions of the Masoretic accents constitute an integrated system with a unified purpose, and that, in essence, neither the system nor the purpose is linguistically "peculiar". I assume that the Masoretes intended the accents to help convey the sense of the text, *not abstractly but through*

---

⁷⁷Rachel Mashiah, "Parallel Divisional Patterns in Biblical Accentuation in the Twenty-One Prose Books, According to the Leningrad Codex" (PhD diss., Bar-Ilan University, 1995).
⁷⁸Rachel Mashiah, "Parallel Realizations of Dichotomy Patterns in Biblical Accentuation," in *Proceedings of the Twelfth International Congress of the International Organization for Masoretic Studies,* ed. E. J. Revell (Atlanta: Scholars Press, 1996), 59–69 at 60.
⁷⁹Mashiah, "Parallel Realizations," 62.

utterance.... Masoretic accentuation is a system for representing this intonational aspect of the correct recitation of the ... text.[80]

While he agrees that the accents will group words in a syntactic manner, this is not the primary foundation upon which the Masoretes laid out the accents.[81] Rather, the Masoretes aimed at recording the correct performance of the text. "The Hebrew of the Masoretic Biblical text is not a language of ordinary speech but a language of recitation."[82] In place of Wickes's principle of continuous dichotomy, Janis proposes a "countdown rule" that aims to represent speech patterns and does not count every disjunctive accent as "pausal."[83] Rather, the Masoretes grouped words into countdown sequences, of which there may be several in a single verse.[84] On this point Janis and Wickes agree, that the accents are intended to aid the hearer of the biblical text. But the accents are also meant to aid the reader, not just in properly intoning the text, but also in discerning the proper syntactic and semantic sense of each passage.

While Wickes commonly uses the musical nature of the accents to explain certain features, Daniel Weil presents a foundationally musical approach to the accents.[85] He builds on the historical fact that

---

[80] Norman Janis, "A Grammar of the Biblical Accents" (PhD diss., Harvard University, 1987), 10 (emphasis added). Cf. Spanier, *Massoretischen Akzente*, 112.
[81] Janis, "Grammar of the Biblical Accents," 30–31.
[82] Janis, "Grammar of the Biblical Accents," 59.
[83] Janis, "Grammar of the Biblical Accents," 224, 229. Unfortunately Janis writes just before Price's *Syntax*. By not accounting for near and far subordinate accents, as Price does, he understands continuous dichotomy as unnaturally placing the "most important dichotomy ... just before the next-to-last word" (*A Grammar of the Biblical Accents*, 226). This would indeed be unnatural. But taking into account the relationship of near and far subordinate disjunctives, this objection quickly dissolves (see discussion under "Price" above; see also ch. 4 of this dissertation).
[84] Janis, "Grammar of the Biblical Accents," 237.
[85] Daniel M. Weil, *The Masoretic Chant of the Bible* (Jerusalem: Rubin Mass, 1995). Weil's stated aim is to "provide a reconstruction of the original performance of

most people throughout history only ever "heard" the accents, they did not see them. "In their eyes, the system is essentially musical, and its other functions, such as the logico-syntactic function and the localization of stress are subordinate."[86] This conclusion leads him to critique Wickes's model of continuous dichotomy; instead he prefers the idea of "syntactical groupings."[87] Yet, Weil also understand the relationship between accents in terms of hierarchy.[88] And while his term "syntactical groupings" may often provide a better description of what the accents are actually doing with the words, ultimately the concept he articulates does not greatly differ from continuous dichotomy.

B. Elan Dresher contributes a significant article to the massive *Encyclopedia of Hebrew Language and Linguistics* arguing for the prosodic basis of the Masoretic accents.[89] While he concedes that prosody and syntax have significant overlap, he attempts to show how deviations from syntax are not due to logical or semantic considerations,

---

the *te'amim*" (7). Thus, the bulk of the book is devoted to that purpose. But his approach and system do provide an alternative to the prevailing model stemming from Wickes.

[86] Weil, *Masoretic Chant of the Bible*, 4.

[87] Weil, *Masoretic Chant of the Bible*, 42. Weil describes the system of continuous dichotomy and writes, "Undoubtedly this is very unnatural for a hierarchy of pausal forces, since it prescribes a dependency between the grade of pausal force of a given pausal accent and its position relative to other pausal accents" (Weil, *Masoretic Chant of the Bible*, 30). But Wickes requires that the "utmost freedom in application of the dichotomy" be granted to the Masoretes, for in every place their chief objective is to bring out the "sense" of the text (Wickes, *Accentuation of the Twenty-One Prose Books*, 31). When the Masorete places Etnachta in a semantically ripe position, the secondary accents cover the basic logical and syntactic pauses of the verse. That is the beauty of the relative dependency of the accents which Weil finds unnatural.

[88] Weil, *Masoretic Chant of the Bible*, 41.

[89] Dresher has also published his argument in a lengthier format: Dresher, "Prosodic Basis," 1–52.

but prosodic features of the text.⁹⁰ He bases much of the argument in modern language prosodic theory and its application mainly applies to lower level accent formation. He suggests that a prosodic explanation for deviation from the syntax helps to better explain the anomalies of the accent system.⁹¹ While this dissertation does not follow Dresher's formulation, his study represents a noteworthy alternative to the prevailing influence of Wickes.

1.6.5   MAJOR INFLUENCES ON THIS DISSERTATION

Joshua R. Jacobson's *Chanting the Hebrew Bible: The Art of Cantillation* provides much more than melodies; this book constitutes an encyclopedic reference and learning tool. Jacobson effectively fuses syntactical parsing and musical performance into one study. He presents a specific tradition of melodies for chanting the Torah and some other key portions of the Hebrew Bible. The melodies are notated in Western musical form and come with manifold examples for the sake of practice. But Jacobson clearly believes that proper chanting of the text requires a proper understanding of the text. He writes, "The Hebrew Bible is punctuated with an elaborate system of stylized inflections that delineate the most subtle nuances of meaning.... The *te'amim* function as an elaborate punctuation system, a means of parsing the syntax of classical Hebrew."⁹² Thus, Jacobson teaches his readers a system for visually parsing the syntax of the accents and the principles associated with this practice.⁹³ In addition to these two main objectives, this book also

---

⁹⁰Dresher, "The Prosodic Basis," 37.
⁹¹Dresher, "The Prosodic Basis," 48.
⁹²Jacobson, *Chanting the Hebrew Bible: The Art of Cantillation*, 23.
⁹³He credits Israeli scholar Michael Perlman with originating this visual system of parsing accent sentences. See Michael Perlman, *Dappim Lelimud Ta'Amey*

covers a range of other important topics from pronunciation to history to accent transformation. While this book may not provide innovative research into the accent system, it serves as an invaluable modern reference tool for understanding the Masoretic system and how it conveys the sense of the text.

Russell T. Fuller provides the most recent extended treatment of the accents in his *Invitation to Biblical Hebrew Syntax: An Intermediate Grammar*. He presents the accents according to five ranks (emperor, king, prince, duke, count) and according to their near and far subordinates.[94] This presentation includes the basic principles for proper division in the vein of Wickes's principle of continuous dichotomy. But proper division of the accents is only the first step to interpreting the accents. He writes:

> The accents were designed to convey the meaning of the text. The accents disclose the meaning on three levels: *the syntactic, the clausal, and the semantic.* The syntactic operates on a single independent clause, grouping and separating words, phrases, and dependent clauses. The clausal operates on multiple independent clauses, grouping and separating them. Operating on both single and multiple independent clauses, the semantic breaks the normal

---

Ha-Mikra (Jerusalem: Ha-makhon Ha-Yisra'eli Lemusikah Datit, 1962). Perlman also published eight extensive volumes that employ this visual parsing through the entire Torah, Joshua, Psalms, and the Haftarot. Jacobson has made his own developments on Perlman's system to precisely show the various levels of accents. Similar efforts at bracketing the text in order to visually display the syntactical breaks may be found in Spanier (1927) and Breuer (1958). Wickes uses a less intricate system of visual breaks to symbolize the layers of syntactical breaks. His method resembles the insertion of numerous Paseqs labelled d1–d4 after the word bearing a disjunctive accent. Both systems provide a roughly equivalent means of locating the points of disjunction, though Perlman and Jacobson's innovations allow for more rapid appraisal of the relationships between phrases (e.g., nesting, subordination, etc.).

[94]There are only four ranks for the אמ״ת accents. Also, see the previous discussion under Price for explanation of the terms "near" and "far (remote) subordinates."

tendencies and patterns of the syntactic and clausal to bring out the meaning by marking the weightiest words, phrases, and clauses in the verse. The syntactic and clausal represent the usual, the expected, the routine; the semantic represents the fascinating, the interesting, the unexpected.[95]

These three levels of interpretation guide much of this dissertation, specifically the distinction between syntactic and semantic functions of the accents. But Fuller does not just teach the principles of reading the accents, he also provides notes on the use of accents so the reader develops both a sequential and circumstantial view of how the accents work to convey the meaning of the text.

1.7   CONCLUSION

Though modern scholarship often neglects the exegetical insights of the Masoretic accents, this time-honored system helps interpreters by confirming and clarifying the sense of the text. One of the chief means of providing and pointing to the meaning comes through the regular accent patterns. These patterns correspond to various syntactic features of the text and will occasionally diverge to indicate points of semantic interest. This dissertation will explore four such patterns with their regular and divergent examples. These examples will illustrate both the consistency of the Masoretic system, as well as their intentional deployment for the sake of locating meaning in a text.

---

[95]Fuller and Choi, *Biblical Hebrew Syntax*, Accents §9 (emphasis added).

CHAPTER 2
ETNACHTA AFTER DIRECT SPEECH

2.1   INTRODUCTION

The Masoretes designed Etnachta to exert the greatest divisional influence within the confines of the verse.[1] This case study will examine how they employ Etnachta in order to signal the closing boundary of direct speech. At times this placement seems rather routine; at times it seems unbalanced or out of place. But at other times the Masoretes seem to have assigned this accent a special mission which diverges from their common practice. Due to the prevalence of direct speech in Hebrew prose, this accent pattern comes to constitutes a regular landmark of Masoretic accentuation.

2.2   GRAMMATICAL CONSIDERATIONS

Native speakers of any language weave direct and indirect speech into everyday conversation with little thought to their distinctive forms. Direct speech *records* the exact words of a speaker or situation; indirect speech *reports* the words of a speaker or situation, but not always exactly. Direct speech stands syntactically independent; indirect speech remains dependent on the initial clause. In other words, English speakers write down direct speech using quotation marks, whereas indirect speech does not require this punctuation. Modern Israeli Hebrew has adopted this punctuation for use in its writing, but such is

---

[1]This dissertation describes Masoretic work actively (see ch. 1, n. 7).

not the case for biblical Hebrew. In a desire to clarify the sense of the text, the Masoretes accentuate the text with careful attention to quoted material.

In Hebrew prose, direct speech often carries the most important information. Fuller writes with regard to semantic accent placement, "instead of occurring on the clause introducing direct speech, the most logical placement, the strongest accents occur within the direct speech clauses where the meaning is most telling."[2] Jacobson concurs writing, "The quotative frame is usually not independent, but instead is downgraded: subsumed under the first half of the verse. Since the primary focus is on the quotation itself, the main dichotomy will be within the quotation."[3] But, at times, Etnachta does occur at the logical placement between introductory statements and the direct speech itself.[4] Further, as this chapter examines, Etnachta often closes the direct speech when it concludes in the middle of the verse.[5] All of these accent positions will appear in the subsequent study. But the study as a whole does not aim to merely present examples of how the Masoretes accent direct speech. Rather, this study aims to determine if their behavior constitutes an intentional pattern from which they occasionally diverge.

---

[2] Russell T. Fuller and Kyoungwon Choi, *Invitation to Biblical Hebrew Syntax: An Intermediate Grammar* (Grand Rapids: Kregel, 2016), Accents §11.1.
[3] Joshua Jacobson, *Chanting the Hebrew Bible: The Art of Cantillation* (Philadelphia: Jewish Publication Society, 2002), 459.
[4] Fuller and Choi, *Biblical Hebrew Syntax*, Accents §9.B.5.e; Jacobson, *Chanting the Hebrew Bible: The Art of Cantillation,* 461. Jacobson also discusses the cases where a quotative frame occurs at the end of the sentence, for example see Isa 1:20; 66:23; Jer 1:8 (462). But since these examples fall beyond the purview of this study they will not be examined in detail.
[5] Fuller and Choi, *Biblical Hebrew Syntax*, Accents §9.C.2.

Table 1. Accents concluding direct speech

Accent	Verses from Judges
Sof Pasuq concludes direct speech [152x][6]	1:1, 2, 12, 14, 24; 2:3; 3:24; 4:7, 8, 20; 6:10, 12, 13, 14, 15, 16, 18*, 22, 23, 26, 29*, 30, 31, 32, 37, 39; 7:4, 5, 13, 14, 15, 17, 20; 8:5, 6, 7, 9, 15, 18*, 19, 22, 23, 24; 9:2, 3, 20, 29*, 33, 36*, 37, 38, 48; 10:10, 14, 15, 18; 11:2, 6, 7, 8, 9, 10, 12, 13, 27, 35, 36, 37; 12:1, 3, 4, 5**, 13:5, 7, 8, 16, 17, 22, 23; 14:2, 3*, 13*, 14, 15, 16*, 18*; 15:2, 3, 7, 10*, 11*, 12*, 16, 18; 16:2*, 5, 6, 7, 10, 11, 13*, 15, 17, 23, 24, 26, 28; 17:2*, 3, 9*, 13; 18:3, 4, 5, 6, 8, 10, 14, 18, 19, 23, 24, 25; 19:5, 6, 9, 11, 12, 13, 17, 19, 20, 22, 24, 30; 20:3, 7, 10, 18*, 23*, 28*, 32*, 39; 21:1, 3, 5, 7, 11, 16, 18, 19, 22
Etnachta concludes direct speech [55x]	1:3, 7, 15; 3:19*, 20, 28; 4:9, 14, 18, 19, 22; 6:18*, 20, 29*; 7:3, 7, 11, 24; 8:1, 3, 18*, 20, 21, 25; 9:29*, 36*, 54; 13:16; 14:3*, 13*, 16*, 18*; 15:1, 6*, 10*, 11*, 12*, 13; 16:9, 13*, 14, 18, 20*, 25; 17:2*, 9*, 10; 18:2; 19:8; 20:13, 18*, 23*, 28*, 32*; 21:8 [9:38 Etnachta ends a quotation of direct speech within a longer section of direct speech]
Other accents conclude direct speech [11x]	3:19*; 11:38; 12:5**, 6*; 15:6*; 16:2*, 12, 20*, 30; 19:28
Notes: * Indicates that the passage contains two instances of direct speech and may be listed more than once in the chart ** Indicates that the passage contains three instances of direct speech	

---

[6]Sof Pasuq is not properly an accent: (1) it comes after the sentence, not on any specific word; (2) it has no melody as do the other accents. Nevertheless, for pedagogical purposes, this dissertation considers Sof Pasuq within the accent hierarchy as the supreme ruler ("emperor"). It governs the entire verse with Siluq and Etnachta as its subordinates.

2.3 SUMMARY OF DATA

In verses containing direct speech that end mid-verse, the Masoretes generally conclude the direct speech with Etnachta (see table 1). The end of the verse (Sof Pasuq) cuts off direct speech 70 percent of the time in the book of Judges (152x total).[7] The remaining 30 percent of recorded direct speech ends somewhere in the middle of a verse. Etnachta punctuates this narrative feature 25 percent of time (55x), other accents punctuate this feature 5 percent of the time (11x). Therefore, when direct speech ends in the middle of the verse, the Masoretes choose to use Etnachta to signal this significant narrative feature 83 percent of the time (i.e., the end of direct speech generally coincides with the most significant verse disjunction). But the situation proves more complex than these simple statistics indicate.

Many passages where direct speech ends in the middle of the verse also contain a second passage of direct speech. Thus, the verse contains two complete passages of direct speech, one of them ending mid-verse. Because Etnachta commonly divides verses into two logically coherent portions, episodes of double quotation could appear to skew the data in favor of Etnachta ending direct speech mid-verse. But, to the contrary, if such double quotation verses are removed from the data pool, the statistics actually slant further in favor of Etnachta being the Masoretic choice for concluding direct speech mid-verse. Thirty-seven verses contain a single instance of direct speech ending in the middle of the verse. Etnachta stands at this conclusion 89 percent of the time, compared to 11 percent by other accents. The four verses

---

[7]See table 1 for a list of the verses that make up each category. Percentages here have been rounded no more than 0.5 percent for the sake of simplicity. All statistics are related to the book of Judges alone and will not be qualified as such.

where another accent concludes the mid-verse direct speech all exhibit clear reasons for diverging from this pattern (Judg 11:38; 16:12, 30; 19:28). Thus, the Masoretes intentionally choose to conclude direct speech ending mid-verse with Etnachta.

2.4 OUTLINE OF THE MASORETIC PATTERN

Etnachta exerts the strongest disjunctive influence within a verse. Often it will break a verse into two portions of roughly equivalent length. But the Masoretes do not focus mainly on equal length when positioning Etnachta.[8] Rather, the sense of the verse dictates the placement of various disjunctive markers, and no less so with Etnachta. Thus, readers can discern Masoretic intentionality by identifying various accents placed according to sense which may appear to leave a "lopsided" dichotomy. For Etnachta this intentionality appears most prominently when the accent is located near the beginning or end of a verse. The following examples will illustrate both Masoretic intentionality and the pattern of concluding direct speech with Etnachta in the middle of a verse.[9]

---

[8]Wickes's law of continuous dichotomy can easily be misunderstood to include only logical breaks in the verse. His "dichotomy" does not refer to two equal portions, though numerous examples of such halving exist. Rather, Wickes writes, "In their desire to mark emphasis, they did not scruple to pass over the most prominent logical pauses. (These pauses were indeed marked by musical pauses, but the *main musical pause* was reserved for the emphasis)" (William Wickes, "A Treatise on the Accentuation of the Twenty-One So-Called Prose Books of the Old Testament [טעמי כ״א ספרים]," in *Two Treatises on the Accentuation of the Old Testament,* ed. Harry M. Orlinsky [New York: KTAV, 1970], 33).

[9]All biblical examples will appear in tables and the discussion will refer to them by their biblical reference location, not usually by table number.

2.4.1 Basic Examples of the Pattern

The least persuasive examples have only two main verbs outside the direct speech (usually *vav* consecutives). The text introduces the direct speech (verb one), quotes the direct speech, and then provides a follow-up action (verb two). Since the direct speech should naturally be grouped with the introduction to the speech, Etnachta falls after the direct speech.[10] This pattern creates two distinct sense units: (A) speech unit—introduction and recorded speech; (B) follow-up action or commentary by the narrator. Even if the text describes the follow-up action very briefly, the natural position for Etnachta still resides at the conclusion of the direct speech.[11] In other words, it is highly unlikely that the Masoretes would break the introduction from the recorded speech, or split the speech with Etnachta, when a follow-up comment exists in the verse.[12]

In Judges 6:20, the follow-up action only consists of two words (20e), compared with twelve in the preceding half-verse.[13] Nevertheless, the most natural break for Etnachta still resides at the end of the direct

---

[10]Wickes, "Accentuation of the Twenty-One Prose Books," 35.

[11]In all the charted examples, direct speech is indented. Other syntactical features are also indented, such as grounding clauses, protasis clauses, parenthetical clauses, etc. A downward facing arrow indicates that the clause is subordinate to that which follows (see especially ch. 4 of this dissertation). This charting approach is a modified form of the text hierarchy scheme presented in Duane A. Garrett and Jason S. DeRouchie, *A Modern Grammar for Biblical Hebrew* (Nashville: B&H, 2009).

[12]Wickes, "Accentuation of the Twenty-One Prose Books," 37.

[13]When the Masoretes join words with Maqef, those words count as one word. See Israel Yeivin, *Introduction to the Tiberian Masorah*, trans. E. J. Revell (Missoula, MT: Scholars Press, 1980), 228–35; Jacobson, *Chanting the Hebrew Bible: The Art of Cantillation*, 329; Fuller and Choi, *Biblical Hebrew Syntax*, Accents §8.A.

speech, holding it together with the introductory statement.[14] While such examples show Etnachta in an unbalanced position, the Masoretes have still employed it in the most logical location. So, though these examples perfectly conform to the Masoretic pattern, they do little to demonstrate that this constitutes an intentional placement.

Table 2. Pattern example: Judges 6:20

(A) Introduction to Speech	וַיֹּאמֶר אֵלָיו מַלְאַךְ הָאֱלֹהִים	20a
Direct Speech	קַח אֶת־הַבָּשָׂר וְאֶת־הַמַּצּוֹת	20b
Direct Speech	וְהַנַּח אֶל־הַסֶּלַע הַלָּז	20c
Direct Speech [Etnachta]	וְאֶת־הַמָּרַק שְׁפוֹךְ	20d
(B) Follow-up Action	וַיַּעַשׂ כֵּן׃	20e

The introduction of a third main verb outside the direct speech adds another layer of complexity and better displays the intentional choices of the Masoretes. The following example provides an instance where such a conscious choice must be made. In Judges 15:1, Samson returns to his wife and father-in-law's house to make amends. The first two clauses set up the direct speech by Samson. Etnachta falls on the end of the direct speech (1d), thus keeping it together with the preceding clauses. Etnachta could also have been located at the end of the initial action statement (1b). This would tie Samson's speech closer to the contrasting action of his former father-in-law. But, since direct speech most commonly continues to the end of the verse, placing Etnachta after

---

[14] See also Judg 1:3; 17:10 for more examples of direct speech with a short follow-up action.

עִזִּים would have left the reading open to confusion.[15] By placing Etnachta after the direct speech the Masoretes both signal the end of Samson's words and present a clear contrast with the final clause.[16]

Table 3. Pattern example: Judges 15:1

Temporal Introduction	וַיְהִ֤י מִיָּמִים֙ בִּימֵ֣י קְצִיר־חִטִּ֔ים	1a
Initial Action	וַיִּפְקֹ֨ד שִׁמְשׁ֤וֹן אֶת־אִשְׁתּוֹ֙ בִּגְדִ֣י עִזִּ֔ים	1b
Introduction to Speech	וַיֹּ֕אמֶר	1c
Direct Speech [Etnachta]	אָבֹ֥אָה אֶל־אִשְׁתִּ֖י הֶחָ֑דְרָה	1d
Follow-up Action (contrast)	וְלֹֽא־נְתָנ֥וֹ אָבִ֖יהָ לָבֽוֹא׃	1e

The previous examples included passages where Etnachta breaks off a short, follow-up action after the direct speech. The Masoretes also used Etnachta to break the direct speech early in the verse. In such cases multiple clauses follow the Etnachta break, many of which would make legitimate choices for the positioning of Etnachta. But the Masoretes consistently reserve Etnachta for the conclusion of direct speech. In Judges 8:20, the verse begins with an introduction to direct speech and a very short imperative. Etnachta breaks the direct speech from the following clause and its grounding statements. This appears to be a

---

[15] See ch. 5 of this dissertation for a discussion of contrast clauses. The contrast (break) structure of Judg 15:1e works to slow down the reading. The break prevents readers from assuming a simple narrative progression of events and forces them to reconsider the relationship between the clauses. Thus, the Masoretic placement of Etnachta naturally conforms to both of these conventions—the end of direct speech and the contrast structure—to indicate a break in the narrative.

[16] See also Judg 3:20; 19:8 for more examples containing direct speech where Etnachta could logically be placed on another clause.

logical placement as it breaks the verse into two roughly equivalent lengths and keeps the grounding clauses (20d, e) with their head clause (20c). This placement also provides a stark contrast for the negative response to the imperative. When a number of clauses follow direct speech, the opportunity for Masoretic choice multiplies. Nevertheless, in this verse they maintain their practice of concluding mid-verse direct speech with Etnachta since no later clause exhibits the strength to draw away the main accent.[17]

Table 4. Pattern example: Judges 8:20

Intro to DS	וַיֹּאמֶר לְיֶתֶר בְּכוֹרוֹ	20a
Direct Speech [Etnachta]	קוּם הֲרֹג אוֹתָם	20b
Follow-up Action (contrast)	וְלֹא־שָׁלַף הַנַּעַר חַרְבּוֹ	20c
Ground #1	כִּי יָרֵא	20d
Ground #2	כִּי עוֹדֶנּוּ נָעַר:	20e

2.4.2 THE PATTERN AND CHARACTER SWITCHING

The perseverance of this pattern persists despite a wide variety of surrounding influences. All of the examples provided thus far show Etnachta at the end of a direct speech unit, but each one also transitions characters at the main dichotomy. Judges 1:3 provides a similar example of character transition immediately following the conclusion of direct

---

[17] See also Judg 8:21, 25 for more examples direct speech with multiple options for subsequent placement of Etnachta. An intriguing example arises in Judg 15:6 where the first episode of direct speech ends so early that the Masoretes use Etnachta to conclude the second episode of direct speech, which is then succeeded by other follow-up actions.

speech, which also hosts Etnachta. In this example, the first character (Judah) makes a request of the second character (Simeon). The two main verbs outside direct speech record one action by each character. If this verse were restated as indirect speech, the two main movements become even clearer: "Judah requested that he and Simeon work together to conquer their territories, and Simeon agreed." The placement of the comma in English divides two statements which could stand on their own. Instead, these statements are joined into one sentence to tie their meaning closer together. In Judges 1:3, the Masoretes perform a similar act of punctuation, except that their verse presents the speech as a quotation.

Table 5. Pattern example: Judges 1:3

Intro to DS (Character #1)	וַיֹּאמֶר יְהוּדָה לְשִׁמְעוֹן אָחִיו	3a
Imperative/Request	עֲלֵה אִתִּי בְגוֹרָלִי	3b
Cohortative	וְנִלָּחֲמָה בַּכְּנַעֲנִי	3c
Future Result [Etnachta]	וְהָלַכְתִּי גַם־אֲנִי אִתְּךָ בְּגוֹרָלֶךָ	3d
Response (Character #2)	וַיֵּלֶךְ אִתּוֹ שִׁמְעוֹן׃	3e

But the character does not need to change for the Masoretic pattern to prevail. In fact, many verses contain both the words and actions of just one character. The following example from Judges 4:9 illustrates this in the ministry of Deborah. The structure mirrors Judges 1:3, but the speaking and the subsequent actions are performed by the same character. Thus, this verse more clearly demonstrates that the conclusion of direct speech dictates the placement of Etnachta. The verse opens with her response to Baraq, and then turns to her follow-up actions based on what she said. But throughout this verse, only one character acts and speaks. The narrator introduces Deborah's speech (9a) and then describes her subsequent actions (9e, f). The quotation provided continues from the introduction to direct speech and ends with Etnachta (9d). Thus, Etnachta keeps the quoted words with the introduction to direct speech in the first half-verse and lets the subsequent actions fill the second half-verse. This same structure occurred in Judges 1:3, only here the actor stays the same throughout. So, while the actor may frequently change after the conclusion of direct speech, this cannot be the main cause determining the position of Etnachta.[18]

Table 6. Pattern example: Judges 4:9

Intro to DS	וַתֹּאמֶר	9a
Intended Action	הָלֹךְ אֵלֵךְ עִמָּךְ	9b
Contrast Clause	אֶפֶס כִּי לֹא תִהְיֶה תִּפְאַרְתְּךָ עַל־הַדֶּרֶךְ	9c
	אֲשֶׁר אַתָּה הוֹלֵךְ	
Grounding Clause	כִּי בְיַד־אִשָּׁה יִמְכֹּר יְהוָה אֶת־סִיסְרָא	9d
Follow-up Actions	וַתָּקָם דְּבוֹרָה	9e
	וַתֵּלֶךְ עִם־בָּרָק קֶדְשָׁה:	9f

---

[18] See the discussion of transition between characters in ch. 3 of this dissertation (cf. Judg 17:3).

2.4.3 The Pattern Across Verses

One more context aids in clarifying that the Masoretes intentionally deploy Etnachta at the conclusion of direct speech. Quotations commonly extend beyond the boundaries of a single verse. Most often they conclude with the Sof Pasuq of another verse (e.g., Judg 7:17–18; 9:7–20; 11:15–27). But at times the Masoretes will conclude longer quotations mid-verse and use Etnachta to punctuate this conclusion. The direct speech in this example from Judges 7:9–11 spans three verses. The quotation begins with a command (9c, d) and encouraging rationale (9e). The next verse contains a conditional statement which nicely conforms to that accent pattern (see ch. 4 of this dissertation). The final verse describes the results that come from obedience to the command (11a–c). But the Masoretes saved the last clause, Gideon's response to God's word, for the end of the verse after Etnachta. Thus, by using Etnachta to conclude three verses of direct speech, the response clause remains closer to the speech and does not begin a new verse.

These examples from the book of Judges demonstrate the Masoretic pattern for concluding mid-verse direct speech with Etnachta and illustrate various contexts in which it operates. The strongest examples contain multiple clauses outside the direct speech and provide alternate choices for the location of Etnachta. Despite multiple choices, changes of character, and lengthy passages of speech, the Masoretes maintain their pattern with remarkable consistency.

Table 7. Pattern example: Judges 7:9–11

Setting	וַיְהִי֙ בַּלַּ֣יְלָה הַה֔וּא	9a
Intro to DS	וַיֹּ֧אמֶר אֵלָ֛יו יְהוָ֖ה	9b
Imperative	ק֥וּם	9c
Imperative	רֵ֖ד בַּֽמַּחֲנֶ֑ה	9d
Grounding Clause	כִּ֥י נְתַתִּ֖יו בְּיָדֶֽךָ׃	9e
Protasis Clause	וְאִם־יָרֵ֥א אַתָּ֖ה לָרֶ֑דֶת	10a
Apodosis Clause	רֵ֥ד אַתָּ֛ה וּפֻרָ֥ה נַעַרְךָ֖ אֶל־הַֽמַּחֲנֶֽה׃	10b
Result	וְשָֽׁמַעְתָּ֙ מַה־יְדַבֵּ֔רוּ	11a
Result	וְאַחַר֙ תֶּחֱזַ֣קְנָה יָדֶ֔יךָ	11b
Result [Etnachta]	וְיָרַדְתָּ֖ בַּֽמַּחֲנֶ֑ה	11c
Response	וַיֵּ֤רֶד הוּא֙ וּפֻרָ֣ה נַעֲר֔וֹ אֶל־קְצֵ֥ה הַחֲמֻשִׁ֖ים אֲשֶׁ֥ר בַּֽמַּחֲנֶֽה׃	11d

2.5   DIVERGENCE FROM THE PATTERN

Four passages in Judges diverge from the pattern of Etnachta concluding direct speech mid-verse (i.e., direct speech does not conclude at the major verse division).[19] At times the Masoretes have to decide between accenting according to their typical pattern or diverging

---

[19]For this summary, only the four examples where a single line of direct speech is marked by alternative accents will be examined. As seen in table 1, more exceptions exist where alternative accents end direct speech mid-verse. But all these other examples occur in verses containing multiple passages of direct speech. Since such passages are less valuable for discerning masoretic intentionality, they are not examined in detail.

from the pattern for the sake of another feature in the text. When they choose against the pattern of Etnachta after direct speech, the direct speech usually receives the next strongest disjunctive accent (e.g., Zaqef, Segol). The following examples illustrate some causes of divergence from the pattern already outlined, as well as illustrating how strong, secondary disjunctives conclude direct speech without fail.

This first divergent passage, Judges 11:38, contains a dramatic one word quotation. The Jephthah narrative has reached its tragic climax: he must slay his daughter in order to keep his vow to God.

Table 8. Divergence example: Judges 11:38

Intro to DS (Character A)	וַיֹּ֫אמֶר	38a
Direct Speech [Zaqef]	לֵ֑כִי	38b
Action #1 (Character A) [Etnachta]	וַיִּשְׁלַ֤ח אוֹתָהּ֙ שְׁנֵ֣י חֳדָשִׁ֔ים	39c
Action #2 (Character B)	וַתֵּ֤לֶךְ הִיא֙ וְרֵ֣עוֹתֶ֔יהָ	39d
Action #3 (Character B)	וַתֵּ֥בְךְּ עַל־בְּתוּלֶ֖יהָ עַל־הֶהָרִֽים׃	39e

In this verse the Masoretes choose to use Etnachta to mark the transition from Jephthah's action (38c) to that of his daughter (38d). Jephthah's initial speech consists of one short imperative to his daughter (38b). The word of command and the action of sending away are one simultaneous event, hence they should logically be grouped together. Placing Etnachta after the imperative would divide these two clauses. Further, the brevity of the command (2FS), the subsequent action being communicated with a *vav*-consecutive (3MS), and the pausal form of the command all provide sufficient indication of where the speech concludes without the use of Etnachta. Nevertheless, this imperative still receives the biggest accentual break within the first half-verse (38a–c). Thus, the Masoretes find fertile syntactic grounds for diverging from their common pattern.[20]

But this reshuffling of the accents, while syntactically sound, also possibly arises from the semantic weight of this verse. Herein resounds a dramatic pause: Jephthah has sentenced his daughter to death with two short months to live [pause]. While the Masoretes could have followed their typical pattern for mid-verse direct speech, the semantic nature of the verse weighs more heavily and draws the stronger accent to the dramatic pause. The Masoretes were able to employ Etnachta semantically in this verse because the direct speech was sufficiently delimited by the terse nature of the statement, the surrounding grammar, and another strong accent available in the place of Etnachta. But if readers are not aware of the typical Masoretic pattern, they will likely miss this semantic arrangement of the accents.

In Judges 11:38, the Masoretes used Etnachta to communicate a logical transition between characters at a climactic moment in the story,

---

[20]It is worth noting the chiastic structure of the verse: Jephthah's speech-act (38a, b), Jephthah's action (38c), his daughter's action (38d), his daughters "speech-act" (38e). This structure positions Etnachta at the crux of the chiasm. While such an interpretation has validity, chiasms remain notoriously subjective (Duane A. Garrett, *Rethinking Genesis: Sources and Authorship for the First Book of the Pentateuch* [Grand Rapids: Baker, 1991], 114). He offers this caution when examining chiastic material in a text:

> Chiastic ... structures should not dominate exegesis. Although chiasmi are sometimes significant, they are sometimes subtle demonstrations of the narrator's skill, which are interwoven well beneath the surface of the text. They do not always indicate where the climax of a text lies. The actual narrative structure although it may correspond exactly to an underlying chiasmus, may be independent of it.

So, this observation should only be considered alongside the other rationale offered in the body of this dissertation.

likely a semantic pause. But they can also use Etnachta for syntactic purposes that weigh more heavily on the meaning than the pattern for concluding mid-verse direct speech. Parenthetical comments are often marked syntactically through the use of a nominal clause. When the subject precedes the verb, or the clause is verbless, it is a nominal clause.[21] In Judges 16:12, the initiator, הארב (the ambush), immediately follows the conjunction *vav* (12e).[22] The author then uses a descriptive participle to announce something about הארב.

Table 9. Divergence example: Judges 16:12

Action #1	וַתִּקַּח דְּלִילָה עֲבֹתִים חֲדָשִׁים	12a
Action #2	וַתַּאַסְרֵהוּ בָּהֶם	12b
Introduction to Speech	וַתֹּאמֶר אֵלָיו	12c
Direct Speech [Zaqef]	פְּלִשְׁתִּים עָלֶיךָ שִׁמְשׁוֹן	12d
Parenthesis [Etnachta]	((וְהָאֹרֵב יֹשֵׁב בֶּחָדֶר))	12e
Follow-up Action #1	וַיְנַתֵּק אֶת הַמֵּיתָרִים מֵעַל זְרֹעֹתָיו כַּחוּט׃	12f

The Masoretes accent parenthetical clauses by placing the remote subordinate disjunctive just before the parenthesis, and placing the governing disjunctive at the end of the parenthesis.[23] In this case the

---

[21]Fuller and Choi, *Biblical Hebrew Syntax*, Syntax §11.A.

[22]See ch. 5 of this dissertation for more on *vav* + X + verb constructions. This break structure serves multiple functions in the text which must be determined contextually. In this verse the narrator breaks into the action to offer some background information.

[23]Fuller and Choi, *Biblical Hebrew Syntax*, Accents §9.C.2.c.

preceding clause concludes with Zaqef (12d), the remote subordinate to Etnachta. The Masoretes prioritize using Etnachta for this parenthetical construction over the conclusion of direct speech.[24] The direct speech still concludes with the most significant disjunctive accent of its unit (Zaqef) which could have conceivably been placed elsewhere (e.g., בהם in 12b). Instead, Zaqef is delayed until the end of direct speech (12d) and Etnachta encloses the parenthetical nominal clause (12e). Once again, the syntax and the accents work together to indicate the conclusion of direct speech, while simultaneously allowing Etnachta to highlight another significant literary feature.

Table 10. Divergence example: Judges 16:30

Introduction to Speech	וַיֹּאמֶר שִׁמְשׁוֹן	30a
Direct Speech [Segol]	תָּמוֹת נַפְשִׁי עִם־פְּלִשְׁתִּים	30b
Action #1	וַיֵּט בְּכֹחַ	30d
Action #2 [Etnachta]	וַיִּפֹּל הַבַּיִת עַל־הַסְּרָנִים וְעַל־כָּל־הָעָם אֲשֶׁר־בּוֹ	30d
Narrator Commentary	וַיִּהְיוּ הַמֵּתִים אֲשֶׁר הֵמִית בְּמוֹתוֹ רַבִּים מֵאֲשֶׁר הֵמִית בְּחַיָּיו׃	30e

The previous passages provided examples of logical, syntactic, and semantic uses for Etnachta where the Masoretes prioritized another literary feature over the conclusion of direct speech. But they never left

---

[24]While this is technically true, the parenthetical nominal clause does not advance the action of the narrative. Thus, in one sense the Etnachta does conclude direct speech, but it does so by including a parenthetical clause describing the situation surrounding that speech.

the ending of direct speech in doubt, it was always marked with the strongest disjunctive available. Judges 16:30 provides another example of the semantic use of Etnachta where the Masoretes take care to conclude direct speech with a strong disjunctive accent. In this case they conclude the direct speech with Segol, the strongest disjunctive in the Etnachta unit (30c).[25] The following Zaqef, though equally strong, is relatively diminished in its disjunctive strength coming subsequent to Segol (30c).[26] The Masoretes choose to save the strongest disjunctive for the most climactic clause in the verse—when the temple falls on all the Philistines and their leaders who had gathered for the revelry (30d). Such a dramatic pause provides the perfect opportunity for the narrator to introduce a concluding summary of Samson's final act of judgment. The Masoretes could easily have placed the Etnachta at the conclusion of the direct speech and still properly divided the syntax of the final clauses using other accents. Instead they go against their normal pattern in order to highlight the literary climax of this entire story.

A final example of divergence from the Masoretic pattern of placing Etnachta on the conclusion of mid-verse direct speech occurs at another climactic event in the narrative. Judges 19:28 records the sad events of very dark days in Israel.

---

[25]The accent Segol shares a name with the vowel. They use a similar symbol of three dots which invert to distinguish the symbols. Wickes also lists alternative names: Segolta, Segulah. These three points are thought to be superior to the two points of Zaqef. But the superiority actually comes from Segol's position before Zaqef in the sequence of the verse (Wickes, "Accentuation of the Twenty-One Prose Books," 61–62).

[26]Fuller and Choi, *Biblical Hebrew Syntax*, Syntax §3.B.n11. Jacobson calls these "stepping segments," each technically of the same disjunctive value but slightly diminished due to repetition and relative position (*Chanting the Hebrew Bible: The Art of Cantillation*, 75).

Table 11. Divergence example: Judges 19:28

Introduction to Speech	וַיֹּאמֶר אֵלֶיהָ	28a
Direct Speech [Tipecha]	קוּמִי וְנֵלֵכָה	28b
Narrator Comment [Etnachta]	וְאֵין עֹנֶה	28c
Action #1	וַיִּקָּחֶהָ עַל־הַחֲמוֹר	28d
Action #2	וַיָּקָם הָאִישׁ	28e
Action #3	וַיֵּלֶךְ לִמְקֹמוֹ:	28f

After the men of Gibeah abuse the Levite's concubine all night, she manages to make it back to the doorstep of the house where her master is staying. In the morning he stumbles over her on his way out of the house. The narrator has intentionally left her status in question, but her failure to respond confirms that she is dead (29c). This moment in the narrative receives the strongest disjunctive accent in order to highlight the horrifying revelation, "And there was no answer" [pause]. Nevertheless, true to form, the preceding direct speech is also marked with the strongest disjunctive in the Etnachta unit, in this case, Tipecha. Thus, the relative levels of the accents leave no doubt as to the limit of the direct speech, while still using the strongest accent to highlight a shocking turn in the story. Once again, the Masoretes prove consistent in both employing and diverging from their typical pattern of accentuation.

2.6 CONCLUSION

The Masoretes conclude mid-verse direct speech in a predictable manner. In the book of Judges they mark such passages with Etnachta

83 percent of the time, and 89 percent of the time when only considering passages with a single unit of direct speech. This chapter has demonstrated that such a practice is an intentional Masoretic choice by highlighting examples where Etnachta occurs near the beginning or end of the verse, preferably with more than two main clauses outside the direct speech. This study included a few very basic examples (Judg 6:20; 8:20; 15:1), but also offered examples that show character changes do not necessarily influence this choice of placement (Judg 1:3; 4:9). Further, it provided one of many passages where the direct speech extends beyond the verse boundary and yet ends in the middle of another verse with Etnachta (Judg 7:9–11). This consistency and predictability in maintaining a pattern of accentuation serves to clarify and confirm the sense of the text.

This study further demonstrates from the divergences that the Masoretes were free to use Etnachta to mark more semantically significant features even when direct speech ends mid-verse (Judg 11:38; 16:30; 19:28). Yet in such situations they also consistently mark the conclusion of direct speech with the next strongest disjunctive accent. They also diverge from their pattern to maintain other literary features, like parenthesis (Judg 16:12), while doing their best to keep the quotation boundary distinct. One of the greatest values in knowing typical Masoretic accentuation patterns arises from these divergences. Often these divergences function like signal flags, alerting the reader to significant semantic features. Hebrew readers will often see these semantic junctures without the aid of the accents. But knowing the Masoretic accent patterns, and noticing divergence from them, infuses the reader with confidence that they are indeed reading with the ancients.

CHAPTER 3
ETNACHTA BEFORE *VE'ATAH*

3.1   INTRODUCTION

Etnachta builds syntactic divisions between the end of direct speech and the rest of the verse. But this powerful accent can signal many more features of the text. Etnachta also builds syntactic sign-posts to indicate points of transition. Grammatical transitions play a vital role in the effectiveness of communication, both in terms of communicating logical relationships between clauses and in locating meaning. Such transitions also form natural locations for grabbing the attention of readers. Thus, transitions also provide good opportunities to witness the accents mirror the meaning.

3.2   GRAMMATICAL CONSIDERATIONS

The adverb ועתה (*ve'atah,* 'and now') serves as a transitional word in many verses or between verses. At times it highlights a temporal connection between the clauses, and at other times the connection will be logical in nature. Arnold and Choi write that the adverb עתה "typically occurs through the compound form וְעַתָּה and usually indicates a shift in the argument or flow of the discourse without a break in the theme. Frequently, this is also accompanied by a temporal shift as well, when one reflects on past events and commits to present or future action."[1] But such transitions are more than routine. Buth writes that

---

[1] Bill T. Arnold and John H. Choi, *A Guide to Biblical Hebrew Syntax* (New

"וְעַתָּה is often used in Hebrew when *a main point or a new point* is about to be made."[2] Such a marker "often *draws attention* to to the contents of the succeeding sentence(s), affording that sentence(s) greater prominence within its larger context."[3] Thus, ועתה plays the important role of signaling segues and highlighting the heart of a passage. These functions make ועתה a valuable marker for syntax and discourse studies. As the data reveals, the Masoretes also understand the importance of the ועתה transition and use the accents to highlight this lexical signal.

3.3 SUMMARY OF DATA

The Masoretes, time and time again, choose to pair Etnachta with mid-verse occurrences of ועתה.[4] Yet, as a result of its prominent role, ועתה occurs less frequently in the middle of the verse. Only 59 out of 171 instances of ועתה in Genesis to Kings occur in the middle of a verse (34.5 percent).[5] Nevertheless, when this feature does occur mid-verse,

---

York: Cambridge University Press, 2003), §4.2.14.b. See also Bruce K. Waltke and Michael P. O'Connor, *An Introduction to Biblical Hebrew Syntax* (Winona Lake, IN: Eisenbrauns, 1990), §39.3.4.f; David Stec, Siam Bhayro, Jacqueline C. R. de Roo, and Helen Spurling, "עַתָּה," in vol. 6 of *The Dictionary of Classical Hebrew,* ed. David J. A. Clines (Sheffield Phoenix, Sheffield, England, 2007), 633–39 at 633 and 636.

[2] Randall Buth, *Living Biblical Hebrew ג: Selected Readings with 500 Friends* (Jerusalem: Biblical Language Center, 2006), 60 (emphasis added).

[3] Christo H. J. van der Merwe, Jackie A. Naudé, and Jan H. Kroeze, *A Biblical Hebrew Reference Grammar* (Sheffield, England: Sheffield Academic, 1999), §11.9 (emphasis added).

[4] To "pair" Etnachta and ועתה simply means that the disjunctive accent concludes the unit preceding the lexical transition. Contrary to ch. 2 of this dissertation, where Etnachta occurred on the final word of direct speech, here the accent does not occur on the focal word but breaks immediately before the word. This study will also commonly state that Etnachta "precedes" ועתה to the same effect. Further, this dissertation describes Masoretic work actively (see ch. 1, n. 7).

[5] The book range Genesis–Kings derives from the basic Hebrew Bible ordering. This represents the core "prose" books of the Torah and the Nevi'im. This

CHAPTER 3: ETNACHTA BEFORE VE'ATAH 55

Etnachta typically pairs with ועתה to signify the most significant mid-verse disjunction. If the data pool is limited to just the book of Judges, Etnachta immediately precedes a mid-verse ועתה formation 71 percent of the time. If the data pool is expanded from Genesis to Kings, Etnachta precedes a mid-verse ועתה formation 80 percent of the time. Thus, the predominant use of Etnachta before ועתה corroborates the understanding that ועתה serves as an important lexical disjunctive. This data also shows that the Masoretes intentionally placed the accents so as to mirror the syntax (see table 12).

For the sake of this study the data pool extended beyond the book of Judges in order to provide sufficient examples with more than two main clauses. The presence of three main clauses in a verse best illustrates the principle that the Masoretes intentionally mark ועתה as a priority disjunction. When the verse contains more than two main clauses, the Masoretes had to make choices about where to place the main break. Main clauses considered here comprise a subject and verb without a preceding subordinate or relative conjunction. The following chart details the verses from Genesis to Kings containing ועתה. Not surprisingly, this adverb always occurs after a major disjunction (i.e., Sof Pasuq, Etnachta, or Zaqef).[6] The relatively few occurrences of ועתה after Zaqef indicates that the Masoretes sought to pair this strong, lexical transition with the strongest possible accentual disjunction.

---

represents a logical place to stop compiling statistics though a full study of all prose texts would be the most comprehensive. But the dividing line between prose and discourse genres grows quite thin in the prophetic books and the writings. This led to the choice to limit the study to book boundaries of the predominantly prose corpus.

[6]Sof Pasuq is not properly an accent: (1) it comes after the sentence, not on any specific word; (2) it has no melody as do the other accents. Nevertheless, for pedagogical purposes, this dissertation considers Sof Pasuq within the accent hierarchy as the supreme ruler ("emperor") with Siluq and Etnachta as its subordinates.

Table 12. Location of ve'atah in relation to the accents

	First Constituent	Following Etnachta	Following Zaqef
Gen	4:11; 20:7; 21:23; 24:49; 27:3, 8, 43; 31:30, 44; 37:20; 41:33; 44:30, 33; 45:5, 8; 48:5; 50:21	3:22; 11:6; 12:19; 30:30; 31:16; 47:4; 50:5	32:11; 50:17
Exod	3:9, 10; 4:12; 5:18; 9:19; 10:17; 19:5; 32:10, 32, 34; 33:13	32:30; 33:5	3:18
Num	11:6; 14:17; 22:6, 19; 24:11, 14; 31:17	22:34	--
Deut	4:1; 5:25; 10:12; 26:10; 31:19	10:22	--
Josh	2:12; 3:12; 9:23, 25; 13:7; 14:10, 12; 22:4; 24:14, 23	1:2; 9:12, 19; 22:4	9:6, 11
Judg	7:3; 9:16, 32; 11:23, 25; 13:4; 20:9, 13	11:13; 13:7; 14:2; 15:18; 18:14	6:13; 17:3
1Sam	6:7; 8:9; 12:2, 7, 13; 13:14; 15:25; 21:3; 23:20; 24:21, 22; 25:7, 17, 26*, 27; 26:19, 20; 28:22; 29:7, 10	2:30; 9:13; 10:19; 12:10; 15:1; 18:22; 19:2; 20:31; 25:26*; 26:8,11,16	20:29
2Sam	2:6, 7; 3:18; 7:8, 25, 28, 29; 12:10, 23, 28; 13:33; 14:15; 17:16; 19:8	4:11; 13:13; 14:32; 18:3; 19:11	13:20; 15:34; 19:10; 24:10
1Kgs	1:12, 18*; 2:9, 16, 24; 3:7; 5:18, 20; 8:25, 26; 12:11; 18:11, 14, 19; 22:23	1:18*	--
2Kgs	3:15; 10:2, 19; 18:23; 19:19	1:14; 3:23; 5:6, 15; 7:4, 9; 9:26; 12:8; 13:19;	--

Note: (No data exists for the book of Leviticus.)
* Indicates more than one use of ועתה in the same verse.

3.4   OUTLINE OF THE MASORETIC PATTERN

The Masoretes intentionally pair mid-verse ועתה clauses with Etnachta. Most ועתה clauses occur as part of recorded speech. In other words, this device rarely resides in the narrator's voice but commonly in the mouths of characters. In general, the Masoretes tend to employ the main accents within the recorded speech, especially when the speech continues to the end of the verse.[7] Thus, they often pass over introductory phrases and even pre-speech actions in order to put the main disjunctions within recorded speech. But within the direct speech multiple options may exist for the placement of the major disjunctive accents.

The author of Judges uses ועתה to transition fifteen times throughout the book. Seven of these uses occur mid-verse, five preceded by Etnachta (11:13; 13:7; 14:2; 15:18; 18:14), two preceded by Zaqef (6:13; 17:3). A few examples will illustrate this pattern, then divergent uses of Zaqef before ועתה will illustrate Masoretic intentionality in accent choice. Other examples from outside Judges assist in illustrating the pattern and divergence from the pattern. First, Judges 13:7 illustrates the Masoretic choice to highlight ועתה and not the subordinate clause. Second, Judges 15:18 illustrates the Masoretic choice to highlight ועתה and not any other verbal clauses. This second example illustrates the pattern more clearly when compared with other texts like 1 Samuel 9:13 and 2 Kings 7:9. These texts represent the general Masoretic pattern for accenting ועתה.

---

[7]Russell T. Fuller and Kyoungwon Choi, *Invitation to Biblical Hebrew Syntax: An Intermediate Grammar* (Grand Rapids: Kregel, 2016), Accents §9.C.1.c.ii. See the latter portion of ch. 2 in this dissertation for further discussion of the relationship between the accents and direct speech.

3.4.1 EXAMPLES FROM THE BOOK OF JUDGES

Samson's mother excitedly reports to her husband the words of the heavenly messenger (Judg 13:7). The angel's message contains three main movements: (1) two predictive clauses, (2) two imperatives, and (3) one subordinate clause. Thus, the Masoretes must choose whether to place Etnachta before the imperatives, before the subordinate clause, or to split any of the clausal pairs. The predictive pair (7b, c) functions as a parallel statement ("conceive," and "give birth") which should be kept together. The same is true for the imperative pair ("drink," and "eat"; 7d, e). The meaning requires that these lines be grouped together unless they represent a point to highlight.[8] Line 7c, therefore, appears to be a very logical placement of the main disjunction. Yet, the Masoretes could have used Zaqef to provide a strong disjunction and save the main break for 7e. This would have grouped the predictions and imperatives in the first half-verse. But according to the accents provided here, the Masoretes group the imperatives (7d, e) and subordinate clause (7f) in the second half-verse; they also highlight the transition signaled by ועתה. Since either option makes logical sense (7c or 7e), it may be the influence of ועתה that draws the strongest accent.

---

[8]The Masoretes will often use the strongest accent to split parallel lines. But this generally occurs in verses where the parallel lines make up most of the content. In this verse there are numerous component parts. Therefore, splitting parallel lines ranks lower on the list of Masoretic priorities. See Fuller and Choi, *Biblical Hebrew Syntax*, Accents §10.

Table 13. Pattern example: Judges 13:7

Intro to Quoted DS	וַיֹּאמֶר לִי	7a
DS—Predictive	הִנָּךְ הָרָה	7b
DS—Predictive	וְיֹלַדְתְּ בֵּן	7c
DS—Imperative	וְעַתָּה אַל־תִּשְׁתִּי ׀ יַיִן וְשֵׁכָר	7d
DS—Imperative	וְאַל־תֹּאכְלִי כָּל־טֻמְאָה	7e
DS—Subordinate Clause	כִּי־נְזִיר אֱלֹהִים יִהְיֶה הַנַּעַר מִן־הַבֶּטֶן עַד־יוֹם מוֹתוֹ׃ פ	7f --

Further in the Samson narrative, another instance of direct speech illustrates the Masoretic preference for pairing ועתה with Etnachta (Judg 15:18). Etnachta again falls at the most logical break in the recorded direct speech.

Table 14. Pattern example: Judges 15:18

Action	וַיִּצְמָא מְאֹד	18a
Intro to DS	וַיִּקְרָא אֶל־יְהוָה	18b
Intro to DS	וַיֹּאמַר	18c
DS	אַתָּה נָתַתָּ בְיַד־עַבְדְּךָ אֶת־הַתְּשׁוּעָה הַגְּדֹלָה הַזֹּאת	18d
DS	וְעַתָּה אָמוּת בַּצָּמָא	18e
DS	וְנָפַלְתִּי בְּיַד הָעֲרֵלִים׃	18f

If the Masoretes had wanted to draw attention to Samson's dire situation, they could have placed Etnachta after 18a. If they had wanted to draw attention to the possibility that Samson would be captured by the Philistines, they could have placed Etnachta after 18e. But the presence of ועתה marks too strong a transition, so the Masoretes match this lexical transition with the major disjunctive accent. While these two examples illustrate the general pattern, stronger examples for Masoretic intentionality exist outside Judges.

3.4.2 Other Narrative Examples

The Masoretes likely choose to place Etnachta before ועתה so often because this transitional word stands at the syntactic crossroads of the verse or extended passage. They consistently choose the point of transition despite the fact that multiple other locations in the verse could work as a major logical break. Two examples from later narrative books further illustrate this principle in action. The writer in 1 Samuel 9:13 records a lengthy string of clauses that break neatly into three sections: the temporal opening (13a–b), the descriptive subordinate clauses (13c–f), and the concluding imperative (13g–h).[9] No natural break arises until the concluding imperative (13g). As an imperative, it draws more attention to itself. Being coupled with ועתה only heightens the focus on this concluding statement. Hence, the Masoretes place the strongest break before this clause. Despite coming so late in the verse, ועתה forms

---

[9]The downward facing arrow in table 15 indicates that the clause depends upon that which follows. Typically indented clauses show their dependence on preceding clauses or the fact that they further elucidate what came before. The downward arrow indicates that the initial clause depends on the following material. In this case, the "when" clause of 13a cannot stand on its own, it must be completed by the "then" clause of 13b (Arnold and Choi, *Biblical Hebrew Syntax*, 5.2.4).

both the strongest and most natural break in the verse; the accents mirror the syntax.

Table 15. Pattern example: 1 Samuel 9:13

Temporal Protasis	כְּבֹאֲכֶ֣ם הָעִ֗יר ↘	13a
Temporal Apodosis	כֵּ֚ן תִּמְצְא֣וּן אֹת֔וֹ	13b
Temporal Indicative	בְּטֶ֨רֶם יַעֲלֶ֣ה הַבָּמָ֘תָה֮ לֶאֱכֹל֒	13c
Subordinate Ground	כִּ֠י לֹֽא־יֹאכַ֤ל הָעָם֙ עַד־בֹּא֔וֹ	13d
Subordinate Ground	כִּֽי־הוּא֙ יְבָרֵ֣ךְ הַזֶּ֔בַח	13e
Subordinate Inference	אַחֲרֵי־כֵ֖ן יֹאכְל֣וּ הַקְּרֻאִ֑ים	13f
Concluding Imperative	וְעַתָּ֣ה עֲל֔וּ	13g
Subordinate Ground	כִּֽי־אֹת֥וֹ כְהַיּ֖וֹם תִּמְצְא֥וּן אֹתֽוֹ׃	13h

The Masoretes also use this principle in 2 Kings 7:9 to highlight the conclusion of a movement within the direct speech. This verse divides into three main sections: a realization (9b–c), a conditional outcome (9d–f), and a chosen outcome (9g–i).[10] The end of the first section (9c) would make a fine semantic placement for Etnachta, thereby separating the outcomes (9d–i) from their initial epiphany (9a–c). But the Masoretes choose to break after the second section, immediately before the ועתה construction (9f). In effect, they tie the conditional closer to the introduction, and they separate the imperatives

---

[10]This passage (cf. Judg 13:7) also illustrates how introductions to direct speech are generally passed over in deciding the placement of the major accents (Fuller and Choi, *Biblical Hebrew Syntax*, Accents §9.C.2).

in a stark juxtaposition. This demonstrates once again the strength of ועתה to locate meaning and draw the main accent break in the verse.

Table 16. Pattern example: 2 Kings 7:9

Intro to DS	וַיֹּאמְרוּ אִישׁ אֶל־רֵעֵהוּ	9a
DS—NC	לֹא־כֵן ׀ אֲנַחְנוּ עֹשִׂים הַיּוֹם הַזֶּה	9b
DS—NC, Ground	יוֹם־בְּשֹׂרָה הוּא	9c
DS—Protasis #1	וַאֲנַחְנוּ מַחְשִׁים	9d
DS—Protasis #2	וְחִכִּינוּ עַד־אוֹר הַבֹּקֶר	9e
DS—Apodosis	וּמְצָאָנוּ עָווֹן	9f
DS—Imperative	וְעַתָּה לְכוּ	9g
DS—Imperative	וְנָבֹאָה	9h
DS—Imperative	וְנַגִּידָה בֵּית הַמֶּלֶךְ׃	9i

These passages from across biblical Hebrew prose exemplify the Masoretic pattern to intentionally pair mid-verse ועתה clauses with Etnachta. This pattern reveals itself most definitively in passages with multiple main clauses, each providing an alternative position for Etnachta to break the verse. Due to the strength of ועתה in transitioning the sentence, the Masoretes mirror the syntactic break with the major accent break. Though this pattern manifests itself overwhelmingly (80 percent from Genesis to Kings), exceptions exist where the Masoreres pair ועתה with Zaqef. But even these divergent examples provide evidence that the Masoretes intentionally pair Etnachta and ועתה wherever possible.

3.5 DIVERGENCE FROM THE PATTERN

The Masoretes diverge from their pattern of pairing mid-verse ועתה with Etnachta for three main reasons: (1) the priority of another pattern; (2) the division of clauses; and (3) a semantic high point in the verse. Each reason for divergence will receive a detailed analysis noting major examples and exceptions.[11]

3.5.1 PRIORITY OF ANOTHER PATTERN

When two syntactical patterns which the Masoretes tend to mark with Etnachta exist in the same verse, they often have to prioritize one over the other. The data from this study reveals two patterns that take precedent over highlighting ועתה in the same verse: (1) the conclusion of direct speech, and (2) the transition between actors in the verse. First, the Masoretic tendency to conclude mid-verse direct speech with Etnachta takes priority over pairing it with ועתה.

Table 17. Divergence example: Genesis 50:17

Quote	כֹּה־תֹאמְר֣וּ לְיוֹסֵ֗ף	17a
Quote (new layer)	אָ֣נָּ֡א שָׂ֣א נָ֠א פֶּ֣שַׁע אַחֶ֤יךָ וְחַטָּאתָם֙	17b
Quote (subordinate)	כִּי־רָעָ֣ה גְמָל֔וּךָ	17c
Direct Speech	וְעַתָּה֙ שָׂ֣א נָ֔א לְפֶ֕שַׁע עַבְדֵ֖י אֱלֹהֵ֣י אָבִ֑יךָ	17d
Action (new subject)	וַיֵּ֥בְךְּ יוֹסֵ֖ף בְּדַבְּרָ֥ם אֵלָֽיו׃	17e

---

[11]Table 12 lists all divergent examples under the column "Preceded by Zaqef."

Genesis 50:17 illustrates an opportunity for the Masoretes to pair ועתה and Etnachta (17c), instead they chose to signal the end of direct speech (17d). Had the Masoretes placed Etnachta at the end of 17c, they would have indicated the conclusion of a quoted speech unit and highlighted the subsequent ועתה-imperative clause. But syntactically they choose to prioritize the end of direct speech in 17d. This divergence from the pattern may also be seen in 1 Samuel 20:29 and 2 Samuel 13:20. Additionally, in 2 Samuel 15:34 the Masoretes choose to break the end of a quoted speech passage rather than highlight the ועתה located within that direct speech. There are no examples where the Masoretes passed over the end of mid-verse direct speech in order to pair Etnachta with ועתה. These examples appear to indicate that the Masoretes chose to signal invisible characteristics, like the conclusion of direct speech, over visible characterstics with lexical representation.[12]

This example from Genesis 50:17 also includes a second structure which the Masoretes prioritized over marking ועתה. When Joseph's brothers conclude their plea for forgiveness the narrator shifts the focus to Joseph's response. So, 50:17d indicates not only the end of direct speech but also transitions to the actions of another character.[13] This second structure, a transition between characters, can also take priority over pairing Etnachta with ועתה in contexts away from the conclusion of direct speech.

---

[12]In other words, ועתה stands at a transition in the text giving it lexical weight and presence; the conclusion of direct speech must be inferred from how subsequent clauses develop, no word by itself signals that transition.

[13]See a similar discussion of this phenomenon in ch. 2 of this dissertation. At times the transition of characters seems to be merely coincidental and not a major feature of the text (cf. Judg 1:3 and 4:9). At other places this transition between characters becomes a highlight point in the verse (Judg 11:38).

Table 18. Divergence example: Judges 17:3

Action—Micah	וַיָּ֛שֶׁב אֶת־אֶ֥לֶף־וּמֵאָ֖ה הַכֶּ֑סֶף לְאִמּ֑וֹ	3a
Action—Mother	וַתֹּ֣אמֶר אִמּ֡וֹ	3b
Speech—Mother	הַקְדֵּ֣שׁ הִקְדַּ֣שְׁתִּי אֶת־הַכֶּסֶף֩ לַיהוָ֨ה מִיָּדִ֜י לִבְנִ֗י	3c
Speech—Mother	לַעֲשׂוֹת֙ פֶּ֣סֶל וּמַסֵּכָ֔ה	3d
Speech—Mother	וְעַתָּ֖ה אֲשִׁיבֶ֥נּוּ לָֽךְ׃	3e

Whereas the transition between characters takes place late in Genesis 50:17, in Judges 17:3 Micah's actions cease early (3a) and give way to recorded speech by his mother (3b–e). In this verse the transition of characters remains distinct from the end of direct speech (3a). The Masoretes employ Etnachta for the character transition but save the next strongest accent break in the passage to pair with ועתה. Notice even how the Masoretes delay the placement of Zaqef by deepening the levels of accents (Pazer and Revia) leading up to the ועתה transition (3b–c). Thus, the Masoretes are able to employ the two strongest disjunctives in the verse on two patterns they typically highlight. This verse provides another example of invisible characteristics (character transition) being prioritized over visible, lexically represented characteristics.

Contrast the example of Judges 17:3 with Judges 18:14. The structure is identical in both passages, but the accents break up the syntax in 18:14 according to different priorities. Etnachta directly precedes ועתה in this verse. The only apparent difference is that the subject has remained the same from the initial action (14a) into the the direct speech (14b).

Table 19. Divergence example: Judges 18:14

Action—Scouts	וַיַּעֲנוּ חֲמֵשֶׁת הָאֲנָשִׁים הַהֹלְכִים לְרַגֵּל אֶת־הָאָרֶץ לַיִשׁ	14a
Action—Scouts	וַיֹּאמְרוּ אֶל־אֲחֵיהֶם	14b
Speech—Scouts	הַיְדַעְתֶּם	14c
Speech—Scouts	כִּי יֵשׁ בַּבָּתִּים הָאֵלֶּה אֵפוֹד וּתְרָפִים	14d
Speech—Scouts	וּפֶסֶל וּמַסֵּכָה	--
Speech—Scouts	וְעַתָּה דְּעוּ	14e
Speech—Scouts	מַה־תַּעֲשׂוּ׃	14f

The first two examples demonstrate that the Masoretes apparently prioritize signaling character transitions with Etnachta over the lexical transition ועתה (Gen 50:17; Judg 17:3). But here, in the absence of a character transition, the Masoretes highlight the next most important syntactic break, the presence of ועתה (Judg 18:14).

But such a conclusion seems unlikely in light of Joshua 9:6 and 9:11. In these parallel passages the Masoretes split the action and the direct speech, though the characters remain the same (contra Judg 18:14). In the process they also seemingly ignore the ועתה division in the direct speech. These two passages undeniably mirror one another as 9:11 recounts the actions of 9:6. Further, the placement of Etnachta before the transition to direct speech is parallel in both passages. Such a small detail must not be overlooked.

Table 20. Divergence example: Joshua 9:6, 11

Action—Gibeon [Etn]	וַיֵּלְכ֣וּ אֶל־יְהוֹשֻׁ֗עַ אֶל־הַֽמַּחֲנֶה֙ הַגִּלְגָּ֔ל	6a
Action—Gibeon [אמר]	וַיֹּאמְר֤וּ אֵלָיו֙ וְאֶל־אִ֣ישׁ יִשְׂרָאֵ֔ל	6b
Speech—Gibeon	מֵאֶ֧רֶץ רְחוֹקָ֛ה בָּ֖אנוּ	6c
Speech—Gibeon [ועתה]	וְעַתָּ֖ה כִּרְתוּ־לָ֥נוּ בְרִֽית׃	6d
Speech—Gibeon [אמר]	וַיֹּאמְר֣וּ אֵלֵ֡ינוּ זְֽקֵינֵינוּ֩ וְכָל־יֹשְׁבֵ֨י אַרְצֵ֤נוּ לֵאמֹר֙	11a
Quote	קְח֨וּ בְיֶדְכֶ֤ם צֵידָה֙ לַדֶּ֔רֶךְ	11b
Quote [Etn]	וּלְכ֖וּ לִקְרָאתָ֑ם	11c
Quote [אמר]	וַאֲמַרְתֶּ֣ם אֲלֵיהֶ֗ם	11d
Quote (new layer)	עַבְדֵיכֶ֣ם אֲנַ֔חְנוּ	11e
Quote [ועתה]	וְעַתָּ֖ה כִּרְתוּ־לָ֥נוּ בְרִֽית׃	11f

The action preceding the verbs of speaking takes significant time to complete. In other words, "the men of Gibeon journeyed to the camp of Israel ... and they spoke." All throughout the Hebrew Bible certain actions occur simultaneous with direct speech, but other actions must be differentiated from the act of direct speech.[14] In this case, Etnachta appears to function in a semantic sense offering a rhetorical pause.[15] The

---

[14] This paradigm of divided action and speech stands in contrast to the more common pairing of an action verb with a concurrent speech verb. Some examples from Judges include יצא in 4:18 and 4:22; פנה in 6:14; and בוא in 8:15.

[15] While this is certainly the least frequent function of the accents, it is by no means a case of special pleading. The Masoretes reserved the right to alter their patterns of clausal and syntactic divisions to draw attention to certain dimensions of meaning. This may be to highlight a climactic point in the narrative (e.g., Judg 16:30), or here the major break may be inserted to ensure a significant pause in the reading.

major disjunction between the action (הלך) and the speech (אמר) signals that they are two independent actions rather than simultaneous.

Though the Masoretes prefer to pair Etnachta with ועתה, they will diverge from their pattern when higher priority formations occur in the same verse. In these cases they always pair ועתה with Zaqef, the strong, remote subordinate of Etnachta and Siluq. Thus, ועתה retains its potency, but another feature of the verse receives the principle syntactic or semantic disjunction. These examples demonstrate how the Masoretes give priority to signaling the conclusion of direct speech (syntax), the change of characters (literary), and points of significant pause in the reading (semantic). Next, this study will explore two other reasons the Masoretes diverge from pairing ועתה with Etnachta.

3.5.2 THE DIVISION OF CLAUSES

The Masoretes use the accents in various ways: to punctuate clauses, to group clauses together, and to highlight semantic points of interest. Often they are doing all three of these in the same verse. But generally one of the three uses for the accents takes precedent for the higher level disjunctives. While the Masoretes prefer to pair ועתה with Etnachta, they do at times choose against this pattern for the sake of clause division. Genesis 32:10 provides an example of such a divergence.

In Genesis 32:10, Jacob exclaims that he is unworthy of God's work in his life (10a). The evidence of this gracious work comes out in the contrast drawn at the end of the verse (10b, c). The Masoretes place Etnachta between these two major constructions rather than in the middle of the contrast. This makes logical sense of the verse. Were they to have paired ועתה with Etnachta, at the end of 10b, then they would have split a contrast pair. While contrast often draws a strong

CHAPTER 3: ETNACHTA BEFORE VE'ATAH   69

disjunctive accent, this would have introduced confusion into the verse since there are only three clauses.[16] Because ועתה often begins a new idea, pairing Etnachta with ועתה in this verse could potentially misdirect readers to see 10a and 10b as a unit, and 10c as a new unit of thought. But since they intend for us to read ועתה as the hinge within the subordinate unit, not the overall verse, they instead pair Zaqef and ועתה. In other words, creating appropriate clause groups remains a higher priority to the Masoretes than a blind commitment to pairing Etnachta and ועתה.

Table 21. Divergence example: Genesis 32:10

Mainline Clause	קָטֹ֜נְתִּי מִכֹּ֤ל הַחֲסָדִים֙ וּמִכָּל־הָ֣אֱמֶ֔ת	10a
Relative Clause	אֲשֶׁ֥ר עָשִׂ֖יתָ אֶת־עַבְדֶּ֑ךָ	--
Subordinate	כִּ֣י בְמַקְלִ֗י עָבַ֙רְתִּי֙ אֶת־הַיַּרְדֵּ֣ן הַזֶּ֔ה	10b
Subordinate	וְעַתָּ֥ה הָיִ֖יתִי לִשְׁנֵ֥י מַחֲנֽוֹת׃	10c

The accents not only generally correspond to clause groupings but also to paragraph divisions. The constraints of these larger forces often require the Masoretes to choose against patterns they would typically highlight with Etnachta. In these parallel passages the paragraph structure breaks differently. The shorter passage in 1 Chronicles omits any reference of David's heart striking him (2 Sam 24:10a). Thus, when the quotation from David constitutes the entirety of the verse, the Masoretes pair ועתה with Etnachta (1 Chr 21:8b). But

---

[16]See ch. 5 of this dissertation for more on the use of accents with contrast structures. See also Fuller and Choi, *Biblical Hebrew Syntax*, Accents §9.C.1.c.ii.

when the Setumah break interposes itself in the middle of 2 Samuel 24:10, then the Masoretes obligingly mark this paragraph division with the strongest accentual break.¹⁷ Such a difference leads to Zaqef as the only option for the ועתה disjunction later in the verse (2 Sam 24:10d).

Table 22. Divergence example: 2 Samuel 24:10 and 1 Chronicles 21:8

1 Chronicles 21:8	2 Samuel 24:10
	וַיַּ֤ךְ לֵב־דָּוִד֙ אֹת֔וֹ
	אַחֲרֵי־כֵ֖ן סָפַ֣ר אֶת־הָעָ֑ם ס
וַיֹּ֤אמֶר דָּוִיד֙ אֶל־הָ֣אֱלֹהִ֔ים	וַיֹּ֤אמֶר דָּוִד֙ אֶל־יְהוָ֔ה
חָטָ֣אתִי מְאֹ֔ד אֲשֶׁ֥ר עָשִׂ֖יתִי אֶת־הַדָּבָ֣ר הַזֶּ֑ה	חָטָ֣אתִי מְאֹ֖ד אֲשֶׁ֣ר עָשִׂ֑יתִי
וְעַתָּ֗ה הַֽעֲבֶר־נָא֙ אֶת־עֲוֺ֣ן עַבְדְּךָ֔	וְעַתָּ֣ה יְהוָ֔ה הַֽעֲבֶר־נָא֙ אֶת־עֲוֺ֣ן עַבְדְּךָ֔
כִּ֥י נִסְכַּ֖לְתִּי מְאֹֽד: פ	כִּ֥י נִסְכַּ֖לְתִּי מְאֹֽד:

This illustrates once again how clause division can take precedent over another pattern of accentuation without ignoring the fact that such a demoted pattern remains a priority.

At times it also appears that ועתה simply exercises less force in the overall discourse. In 2 Samuel 19:10 ועתה introduces a temporal statement that is part of a longer speech extending through 19:11. The ועתה in 19:11 expresses a strong, logical conclusion and draws Etnachta. But in 19:10 the Masoretes place Etnachta on the introduction to direct speech, לאמר ("saying").¹⁸ Jacobson writes that לאמר is

---

¹⁷See Yeivin, *Masorah*, §74.

¹⁸Of the numerous occurrences of לאמר in the Hebrew Bible: 299 times the

"always syntactically separated from the quote that follows. It appears as the last word of the quotative frame, connected to whichever word (or phrase) precedes it."[19] In 2 Samuel 19:10 this syntactic separation features more prominently than the temporal transition provided by ועתה. Further, in the overall direct speech passage of 19:10–11, the main point lies in the question contained in 11b. Though it would make perfect sense for Etnachta to precede ועתה in both verses, perhaps the Masoretes pair ועתה with Zaqef in 10e in order to draw more attention to the ועתה in 11b.[20] In keeping with the way they accent other multi-verse speech units, this would not be surprising.[21] In order to highlight the more important transition in the direct speech (11b), the first occurrence breaks the typical pattern (10e).

Masoretes mark it with Siluq, 219 times with Etnachta, 221 times with Zaqef, 89 times with Revia, and the remainder are quite varied. This wide variety of accents on לאמר are relatively evenly distributed. Thus, while the Masoretes do pair לאמר with the main break, this is statistically far from an intentional pattern.

[19]Joshua Jacobson, *Chanting the Hebrew Bible: The Art of Cantillation* (Philadelphia: Jewish Publication Society, 2002), 478. Jacobson references Cynthia Miller, *The Representation of Speech in Biblical Hebrew Narrative: A Linguistic Analysis* (Atlanta: Scholars Press, 1996), 200. Compare her description of לאמר with Richard Charles McDonald, *Grammatical Analysis of Various Biblical Hebrew Texts According to a Traditional Semitic Grammar* (PhD diss., The Southern Baptist Theological Seminary, 2014), 120–28. See also Waltke and O'Connor, *Biblical Hebrew Syntax*, §36.2.3e; Fuller and Choi, *Biblical Hebrew Syntax*, Accents §9.B.5.e.

[20]Fuller and Choi, *Biblical Hebrew Syntax*, Accents §9.C.2.a. I offer this suggestion tentatively as these two verses are also bracketed by Setumah breaks in the traditional reading, thereby isolating this unit. Verse breaks, reading units, and literary features all contribute to the layout of this passage. Nevertheless, I think it makes good sense of the verse to look for the main point of the entire speech, not just the main point of v.10.

[21]Compare this example to Judg 7:9–11 in ch. 2 of this dissertation and Judg 11:30–31 in ch. 4. In both of these examples the Masoretes maintain their pattern across verse boundaries. In this case with ועתה it seems like they could have kept the pattern up in both verses. But if the message of the entire speech unit is taken into consideration, their choice to diverge on the first occurrence makes much more sense.

Table 23. Divergence example: 2 Samuel 19:10–11

Action	וַיְהִ֤י כָל־הָעָם֙ נָד֔וֹן בְּכָל־שִׁבְטֵ֖י יִשְׂרָאֵ֑ל	10a
Intro to DS	לֵאמֹ֔ר	10b
DS (past action)	הַמֶּ֜לֶךְ הִצִּילָ֣נוּ ׀ מִכַּ֣ף אֹיְבֵ֗ינוּ	10c
DS (past action)	וְה֥וּא מִלְּטָ֖נוּ מִכַּ֣ף פְּלִשְׁתִּ֑ים	10d
DS (status)	וְעַתָּ֕ה בָּרַ֥ח מִן־הָאָ֖רֶץ מֵעַ֥ל אַבְשָׁלֽוֹם׃	10e
DS (status)	וְאַבְשָׁלוֹם֙ אֲשֶׁ֣ר מָשַׁ֣חְנוּ עָלֵ֔ינוּ מֵ֖ת בַּמִּלְחָמָ֑ה	11a
DS (question)	וְעַתָּ֗ה לָמָ֥ה אַתֶּ֛ם מַחֲרִשִׁ֖ים לְהָשִׁ֥יב אֶת־הַמֶּֽלֶךְ׃	11b

3.5.3   Semantic High Points

In addition to the priority of other patterns and clause divisions, the Masoretes also diverge from pairing mid-verse ועתה with Etnachta because of semantic high points in the verse. Semantic high points appear in any verse where the Masoretes employ the major disjunctive to mark the most salient point, instead of a more logical one. But semantic high points take on a new vitality when they occur in climactic contexts, often near the end or major transition in a story. These points of interest will take precedent over any accent pattern typically employed by the Masoretes. The strongest break in the verse, Etnachta, remains the most straightforward manner of signaling semantic high points. Thus, as a result, other priority patterns receive accents one level lower on the hierarchy (e.g., Tipecha, Zaqef). Two possible examples of this paradigm occur in this corpus: Judges 6:13 and Exodus 3:18.

Judges 6:13 provides an example of subtle semantic

displacement. In this verse Etnachta should fall at the end of 13g for two reasons: (1) 13g concludes a quotation within a larger direct speech frame, and (2) 13h begins with ועתה. Chapter 2 already presented how the completion of direct speech draws the strongest accent and displaces other patterns (cf. Gen 50:17; 1 Sam 20:29; 2 Sam 13:20, 15:34). For this reason alone Etnachta should occur at the end of 13g. But the choice to signal a semantic high point supercedes all other patterns, even when two strong accent patterns meet in the same location. Here Gideon inquires of the heavenly messenger about the God's past and future actions. His initial question trumpets, "If YHWH is with us, then why has all this (trouble) found us?"[22] This is a shocking question to ask the messenger of God, especially for someone hiding from his enemies in a wine press. It reveals a raw nerve of anger and discontentment from the lips of the soon-to-be hero.[23] Instead of hiding the brazen nature of Gideon's question, the Masoretes mark the moment with a resounding pause.[24]

---

[22]See ch. 4 of this dissertation for the Masoretic pattern of accentuation on conditional statements. In this case the protasis concludes with Zaqef and therefore the apodosis must conclude with the accent superior to Zaqef, which is Etnachta. But this cannot be the factor determining the position of Etnachta overall because multiple other accentuation options exist for a conditional this early in the verse. The Masoretes choose to place Etnachta on this conditional construction.

[23]Compare this with Daniel I. Block, *Judges, Ruth*, NAC 6 (Nashville: B&H, 1999), 260.

[24]Another Masoretic convention can explain this placement of Etnachta. Often when a list of questions or parallel statements occurs, the Masoretes will split the list using Etnachta. But this pattern does not tend to exert strong influence over other potential points of interest. Since the Masoretes so strongly favor marking the end of quoted speech, this explanation seems unlikely in this case.

Table 24. Divergence example: Judges 6:13

Intro to DS	וַיֹּ֤אמֶר אֵלָיו֙ גִּדְע֔וֹן	13a
Polite Request	בִּ֣י אֲדֹנִ֔י	13b
Q#1: Protasis	וְיֵ֤שׁ יְהוָה֙ עִמָּ֔נוּ	13c
—Apodosis [Etn]	וְלָ֥מָּה מְצָאַ֖תְנוּ כָּל־זֹ֑את	13d
Q#2	וְאַיֵּ֣ה כָֽל־נִפְלְאֹתָ֡יו אֲשֶׁר֩ סִפְּרוּ־לָ֨נוּ אֲבוֹתֵ֜ינוּ	13e
Intro to Quote	לֵאמֹ֗ר	13f
Quoted DS	הֲלֹ֤א מִמִּצְרַ֙יִם֙ הֶעֱלָ֣נוּ יְהוָ֔ה	13g
Conc #1 [ועתה]	וְעַתָּה֙ נְטָשָׁ֣נוּ יְהוָ֔ה	13h
Conc #2	וַֽיִּתְּנֵ֖נוּ בְּכַף־מִדְיָֽן׃	13i

Exodus 3:18 provides an example of stronger semantic displacement. Etnachta occurs on the second word of the verse. This placement indicates certainty on the part of the speaker, "They will listen to your voice!" While a slight shift in subject occurs from 18a to 18b, the collective subject of 18b still contains the subjects of 18a. So, it is possible that a change in characters accounts for the placement of Etnachta, but this seems less likely (cf. Judg 17:3). In fact, 18d creates an ideal setting for Etnachta: it nicely splits the direct speech, it precedes ועתה, and it has its own sense of subtle emphasis. Yet these features combined cannot override the semantic emphasis the Masoretes aim to communicate by fronting Etnachta.

CHAPTER 3: ETNACHTA BEFORE VE'ATAH

Table 25. Divergence example: Exodus 3:18

Action #1 (elders)	וְשָׁמְע֖וּ לְקֹלֶ֑ךָ	18a
Action #2 (+Moses)	וּבָאתָ֡ אַתָּה֩ וְזִקְנֵ֨י יִשְׂרָאֵ֜ל אֶל־מֶ֣לֶךְ מִצְרַ֗יִם	18b
Intro to Quoted DS	וַאֲמַרְתֶּ֣ם אֵלָיו֒	18c
DS—Announcement	יְהֹוָ֞ה אֱלֹהֵ֤י הָֽעִבְרִיִּים֙ נִקְרָ֣ה עָלֵ֔ינוּ	18d
DS—Request [ועתה]	וְעַתָּ֗ה נֵֽלְכָה־נָּ֞א דֶּ֣רֶךְ שְׁלֹ֤שֶׁת יָמִים֙ בַּמִּדְבָּ֔ר	18e
DS—Request (Cont.)	וְנִזְבְּחָ֖ה לַֽיהֹוָ֥ה אֱלֹהֵֽינוּ׃	18f

The Masoretes diverge from their pattern of pairing mid-verse ועתה with Etnachta for three main reasons: (1) the priority of another pattern; (2) the division of clauses; and (3) a semantic high point in the verse. Other patterns, like the conclusion of direct speech or a change of subject, will at times force the Masoretes to prioritize which pattern will receive the major disjunctive accent (Gen 50:17; Josh 9:6,11; Judg 17:3; 18:14). At times the appropriate division of clauses proves more important for a proper reading of the text than following their typical syntactic convention (Gen 32:10; 2 Sam 24:10 and 1 Chr 21:8; 2 Sam 19:10–11). In other verses a major literary feature stands out from passage and the main disjunction functions like a semantic spotlight (Judg 6:13; Exod 3:18). But in all these divergent passages, the Masoretes maintain the practice of clarifying and confirming the sense of the text through the accents.

3.6 CONCLUSION

The Masoretes highlight the presence of ועתה with the strongest accent possible. When ועתה occurs in the middle of a verse, the Masoretes pair Etnachta with this lexical transition 80 percent of the time in narrative texts. Their pattern mirrors the grammatical and syntactic sense of the verse (e.g., Judg 13:7; 15:18; 1 Sam 9:13; 2 Kgs 7:9). It should not surprise Hebrew readers that ועתה functions to begin a new point in the discourse or to highlight the upcoming clause. But the consistency of the Masoretes in breaking the verse before this transition indicates how the accents confirm and clarify the sense of the text.

The Masoretes will diverge from this general pattern for a number of different reasons; yet, each divergence further demonstrates that their general pattern is to pair ועתה with Etnachta. This chapter showed how the Masoretes will depart their pattern in order to (1) employ Etnachta on higher priority patterns (Gen 50:17; Josh 9:6,11; Judg 17:3; 18:14), (2) mark significant clause divisions (Gen 32:10; 2 Sam 24:10 and 1 Chr 21:8; 2 Sam 19:10–11), and (3) highlight semantic points on interest that occur in the same verse (Exod 3:18; Judg 6:13). Even in these cases, the ועתה construction always receives the next most signficant accent break (Zaqef). Thus, the Masoretes clearly demonstrate that they prefer to pair Etnachta and ועתה in the middle of a verse whenever possible; and when it is not possible, to use the next strongest accent available.

The predictability of this pattern, in both normative and divergent forms, creates a useful tool for readers and exegetes. Readers who remain aware of Masoretic patterns for deploying the accents will receive confirmation of grammatical and syntactic structures. When the text presents some more ambiguous situations, awareness of what the

Masoretes choose to do, and what they choose not to do, will clarify the meaning of the text. Further, readers who understand Masoretic patterns will notice when they depart from these conventions, shining light on semantic high points they may not have noticed otherwise. The previous two chapters provided examples of Etnachta employed alongside certain syntactic features. The next chapter will present examples of how the Masoretes use the accents to frame multi-clause syntactic features of the Hebrew text.

CHAPTER 4
ACCENTS FRAMING CONDITIONAL SENTENCES

4.1 INTRODUCTION

Etnachta cannot serve all the Masoretic accent patterns because Etnachta cannot be in two places at once. This dilemma cuts two ways. First, multiple syntactic and semantic features often collide in the same verse. As the last two chapters demonstrated, this forces the Masoretes to choose which pattern will receive Etnachta. Second, many syntactic constructions convey their meaning via multiple clauses. The position of Etnachta cannot exclusively define the pattern for these constructions because multiple accents must frame the syntax. This pattern of accent framing introduces another paradigm for consistent accentuation across the biblical spectrum.

4.2 GRAMMATICAL CONSIDERATIONS

Conditional sentences contribute to the narrative and discourse by means of two clauses: "A conditional clause indicates circumstances under which another clause is true or occurs. It is the 'if' part of an 'if-then' statement."[1] The conditional clause, which generally occurs first,

---

[1] John C. Beckman, "Conditional Clause: Biblical Hebrew," in vol. 1 of *Encyclopedia of Hebrew Language and Linguistics* (Brill: Boston, 2013), 545–48. See also Bill T. Arnold and John H. Choi, *A Guide to Biblical Hebrew Syntax* (New York: Cambridge University Press, 2003), §5.2.2; Russell T. Fuller and Kyoungwon Choi, *Invitation to Biblical Hebrew Syntax: An Intermediate Grammar* (Grand Rapids: Kregel, 2016), Syntax §76–78; Christo H. J. van der Merwe, Jackie A. Naudé, and Jan H. Kroeze, *A Biblical Hebrew Reference Grammar* (Sheffield, England: Sheffield

is also called the "protasis;" the subsequent completion clause is called the "apodosis."[2] Logically speaking, the conditional clause is subordinate to the completion clause.[3] Such sentences may indicate "real" events that could actually happen, or "unreal" events, that which is contrary-to-fact.[4] Hebrew introduces these clauses in a variety of ways. A "real" protasis may begin with *vav*, אם, כי, or אשר. An "unreal" protasis may begin with particles לולא, לוא, לו, or לולי.[5] The apodosis usually begins with a resumptive *vav*, but may also use the particles אז and כי אז.[6] Conditional sentences tend to occur in direct speech and not in the words of the narrator.

4.3   SUMMARY OF DATA

The accents assist the reader in identifying the boundaries of a conditional sentence. Whichever disjunctive accent concludes the protasis, a corresponding accent of higher rank will conclude the apodosis. In other words, the protasis receives the subordinate accent, the apodosis its superior accent. By framing the protasis and apodosis with accents of different ranks, the Masoretes effectively punctuate the

---

Academic, 1999), §12.1, 12.5.3; Bruce K. Waltke and Michael P. O'Connor, *An Introduction to Biblical Hebrew Syntax* (Winona Lake, IN: Eisenbrauns, 1990), §38.2; Ronald J. Williams, *Williams' Hebrew Syntax,* 3rd ed., ed. John C. Beckman (Toronto: University of Toronto Press, 2007), §511–17.

[2]This study will occasionally use the term "conditional," "conditionals," or "conditional statement" as an alternative form for the full protasis-apodosis package. "Protasis" and "apodosis" will be used as terms referring to the individual half-unit.

[3]Biblical reference tables depict this relationship by indenting the conditional clause (protasis) with a downward arrow pointing to the completion clause (apodosis).

[4]Fuller and Choi, *Biblical Hebrew Syntax,* Syntax §76. Generally speaking, unreal conditionals do not describe future events and are rarer than the real variety.

[5]Rare particles include הן for real clauses and אלו for unreal.

[6]Williams, *Hebrew Syntax,* §512.

sentence.[7] In the book of Judges, conditional sentences exhibit this pattern 87 percent of the time (27 out of 31occurrences). Since one of the few divergent examples contains a significant text-critical issue at this point (i.e., the conditional is incomplete), it may properly be removed from the data pool. Thus, conditional sentences in the book of Judges exhibit this accent pattern 90 percent of the time (see table 26).

The regularity of this pattern indicates that the Masoretes made it a syntactical priority. Such regularity also lends itself to predictability, which then benefits the reader. The following examples elucidate the simplicity of this pattern in operation, at the same time portraying the syntactic complexity it can bear. Conditional statements, better than any other example in this dissertation, illustrate how accent patterns work across verse boundaries. This again indicates the complexity that the Masoretes were able to map out using their accent system. As with the other patterns presented here, divergent examples show how the Masoretes occasionally go against their typical pattern. But they only go against a typical pattern with justifiable reason. Though their reasons may be difficult to discern at times, each example of divergence from the general pattern lends more credence to the fact that the Masoretes intentionally frame conditional clauses.

---

[7]This dissertation describes Masoretic work actively (see ch. 1, n. 7).

Table 26. Accents framing conditional sentences

Accents	Conforms to Pattern	Diverges from Pattern
FULL VERSE		
Etnachta—Sof Pasuq[8]	1:12; 6:17; 7:10; 9:19; 11:9; 15:7*; 16:7, 11	—
PARTIAL VERSE		
Pashta—Zaqef	6:31b; 13:16a, 23*; 16:17b	—
Tipecha—Etnachta	4:8a; 13:16b	—
Zaqef—Etnachta	6:13a; 7:3a; 9:15a; 14:13a (Segol)	9:20*
Tipecha—Siluq	4:8b, 20b	—
Zaqef—Siluq	6:37b; 8:19b; 9:15b; 11:10b‡; 14:12b, 18b	16:13†; 21:21* (Segol)
MULTIPLE VERSES		
————	(9:16–19); 11:30–31	6:36–37

Notes:
x* Indicates multiple apodosis statements
x† Indicates a text critical issue (see commentary on verse)
x‡ Indicates a reverse order of protasis-apodosis due to oath formula

---

[8] Sof Pasuq is not properly an accent: (1) it comes after the sentence, not on any specific word; (2) it has no melody as do the other accents. Nevertheless, for pedagogical purposes, this dissertation considers Sof Pasuq within the accent hierarchy as the supreme ruler ("emperor"). It governs the entire verse with Siluq and Etnachta as its subordinates.

4.4 OUTLINE OF THE MASORETIC PATTERN

The hierarchical ranking of the accents has incited continual debate through the centuries of Masoretic scholarship. Samuel Bohlius first articulated a ranking system named after common medieval European classes. This nomenclature has been used by Christian and Jewish scholars alike since his time.[9] Russell Fuller summarizes the hierarchy like this:

> Hierarchy expresses the order of the disjunctive accents. Each lower rank is directly subordinate to its immediate superior: kings are directly subordinate to the emperor, as the princes are directly subordinate to kings, and so forth. Subordinates are divided into near subordinates and remote subordinates. The emperor Soph Pasuq, for instance, has a near subordinate, Silluq, and a remote subordinate, Athnach.[10]

This accent hierarchy corresponds to the syntactic hierarchy of the verse. Price writes, "There is an approximate correspondence between the hierarchy of the accents and the syntactic hierarchy of the language, but the correspondence is relative within the domain of a verse."[11] Conditionals illustrate this principle well. The subordinate accent resides on the initial, subordinate clause; the superior accent resides on the second clause. The lesser accent is on the conditional proper, the

---

[9]William Wickes, "A Treatise on the Accentuation of the Three So-Called Poetical Books of the Old Testament, Psalms, Proverbs, and Job (טעמי אמ״ת)," in *Two Treatises on the Accentuation of the Old Testament,* ed. Harry M. Orlinsky (New York: KTAV, 1970), x. Many resources on the accents present a four-class hierarchy. Sof Pasuq is either grouped with Silluq, considered the *de facto* lord of the sentence, or left out of the scheme entirely since it is not properly one of the *te'amim.* Another rendering of ranks places them in five classes, thus separating Sof Pasuq from Silluq. This study follows the five-rank system in this dissertation for pedagogical purposes. See appendix 1 for a chart of the accents and their hierarchical relationships.

[10]Fuller and Choi, *Biblical Hebrew Syntax,* Accents §2.B.

[11]James D. Price, *The Syntax of Masoretic Accents in the Hebrew Bible* (Lewiston, NY: Mellen, 1990), 139.

greater accent on the completion clause. Thus, the accent hierarchy matches the syntax of the language.

Two relationships stand at the center of the accent hierarchy: (1) *horizontal* relationships between peers of the same rank, and (2) *hierarchical* relationships between accents of different rank.[12] First, horizontal relationships define the near and far subordinates of their accent lord; they create "stepping phrases."[13] Stepping phrases do not change rank but they do grow steadily weaker as they get closer to their lord. Thus, the farther away an accent stands from its lord, the more influence it exerts.[14] In the example from Judges 1:1a, three phrases conclude with level three accents (i.e., Zaqef and Tipecha). Each phrase diminishes in disjunctive potency but does not subordinate itself to its neighbor; all are subordinate to Etnachta (see figure 1).[15]

---

[12] See appendix 1, "Masoretic Accent Hierarchy," for these relationships.

[13] Joshua Jacobson, *Chanting the Hebrew Bible: The Art of Cantillation* (Philadelphia: Jewish Publication Society, 2002), 75.

[14] For example, Zaqef imposes a stronger break than Tipecha when both occur in the same half-verse; if Zaqef is repeated in a half-verse, the first Zaqef constitutes the strongest break in the half-verse. This feature of the accent system allows relatively long statements to remain on the same hierarchical level.

[15] The numbers used in figure 1 refer to the hierarchical levels of these accents (see appendix 1). Tipecha and Zaqef are both level three accents, one the near subordinate of Etnachta, one the far subordinate. Both exercise the same rank within the domain of Etnachta, but the far subordinate (when present) always constitutes that most significant break in the domain of its superior. It may be compared to the medieval titles given these ranks. All three subordinate accents in this example (Tipecha, Zaqef) are princes to the great king (Etnachta). All three possess the same rank, but one prince has preeminence and therefore exercises more influence within the kingdom.

Figure 1. Stepping phrases (Judges 1:1a)

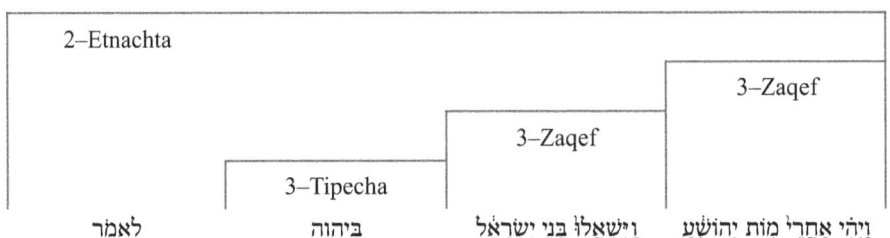

Second, hierarchical relationships define the subordination of certain accents to the realm of their lord; they create "nesting phrases."[16] Nesting phrases constitute a lower rank and exercise their influence only within the realm of their lord.[17] For example, in Judges 1:1b, the three disjunctive accents all nest within one another (see figure 2).[18] Siluq reigns over the whole half-verse, Tipecha reigns within the realm of Siluq, and Tevir reigns within the realm of Tipecha. As another example, figure 1 includes a nested phrase in the first Zaqef segment. Revia (level four) stands over the first word and creates a small nested phrase within the greater Zaqef segment.

---

[16] Jacobson, *Chanting the Hebrew Bible: The Art of Cantillation*, 75. See also Jacobson's summary on p. 84. See also Fuller and Choi, *Biblical Hebrew Syntax*, Accents §9.B.3.

[17] For example, Pashta exercises its authority within the realm of Zaqef, whereas Tevir exercises its authority within the realm of Tipecha. These subordinates rule their own realms which are under the jurisdiction of a higher ranked accent.

[18] Jacobson uses this method of bracketing extensively throughout his book *Chanting the Hebrew Bible*. He bases his system on the work of Michael Perlman. See Jacobson, *Chanting the Hebrew Bible: The Art of Cantillation*, 36. Once again, the numbers with each accent in figure 2 represent its hierarchical level (see appendix 1).

Figure 2. Nesting phrases (Judges 1:1b)

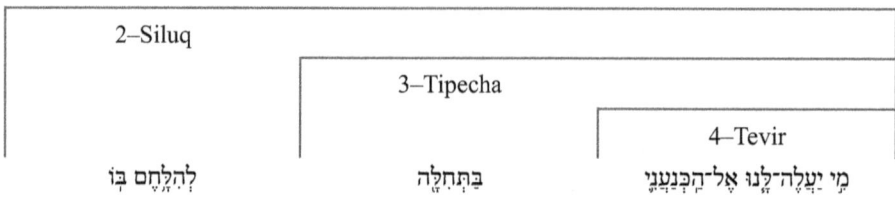

In other words, nested phrases are subordinate to a superior accent, whereas stepped phrases are merely weaker than a neighboring accent. This dimension of the Masoretic system forges a central tenet to the proper parsing of the accents and to understanding the pattern used with conditional clauses.

The Masoretes frame conditional sentences with accents of differing ranks. The protasis concludes with a particular disjunctive accent, and the apodosis concludes with that accent's immediate superior. This pattern will manifest itself in full-verse, half-verse, compound, partial-verse, and multi-verse examples.

4.4.1 Full-Verse Conditional Sentences

Judges 6:17 provides a simple example of a full-verse conditional. The conditional protasis in 17b begins with an אם particle and ends with the accent Etnachta. The apodosis in 17c begins with a *vav* conjunctive and concludes with the accent Siluq. But Siluq fits hand-in-glove with Sof Pasuq, no accent or word ever comes between them. Siluq and Sof Pasuq have a unique relationship. Siluq governs the last half-verse, whereas Sof Pasuq governs the whole verse, yet they occur on the same word. Siluq marks the accented syllable of the last word, Sof Pasuq stands in the final position after the last word. Thus, understanding the relationship between Siluq and Sof Pasuq, full-verse conditionals framed by Etnachta and Sof Pasuq illustrate the pattern.[19]

Table 27. Pattern example: Judges 6:17

Intro to DS	וַיֹּאמֶר אֵלָיו	17a
DS Protasis	אִם־נָא מָצָאתִי חֵן בְּעֵינֶיךָ ↘	17b
DS Apodosis	וְעָשִׂיתָ לִּי אוֹת שָׁאַתָּה מְדַבֵּר עִמִּי׃	17c

4.4.2 HALF-VERSE CONDITIONAL SENTENCES.

Though full-verse conditionals clearly illustrate the pattern, verse termination with Siluq and Sof Pasuq introduces a point of potential confusion.[20] Perhaps even more simple are examples of half-verse conditionals. Conditional statements occur in both the first half-verse and in the second half-verse. At times verses contain multiple conditional clauses that fill out both half-verses. Judges 4:8 provides an example of multiple half-verse conditional sentences framed by the accents.

---

[19] All biblical examples will appear in tables and the discussion will generally refer to them by their biblical reference location, not by table number. For a nearly identical example to Judg 6:17, only without the *vav* conjunctive, see Gen 18:3. The right-downward arrow in the text-hierarchy depiction indicates that the indented line is subordinate to that which follows. Throughout this chapter this arrow typically refers to the protasis/apodosis relationship. For more on text-hierarchy see uane A. Garrett and Jason S. DeRouchie, *A Modern Grammar for Biblical Hebrew* (Nashville: B&H, 2009).

[20] The term "half-verse" refers not to some sort of lexical balance between the halves. Rather, it refers to the two portions divided by the first major disjunctive, usually Etnachta.

Table 28. Pattern example: Judges 4:8

Intro to DS	וַיֹּ֤אמֶר אֵלֶ֙יהָ֙ בָּרָ֔ק	8a
DS Protasis #1	אִם־תֵּלְכִ֥י עִמִּ֖י ↘	8b
DS Apodosis #1	וְהָלָ֑כְתִּי	8c
DS Protasis #2 [contrast]	וְאִם־לֹ֥א תֵלְכִ֛י עִמִּ֖י ↘	8d
DS Apodosis #2	לֹ֥א אֵלֵֽךְ׃	8e

Baraq's hesitancy to follow God's command comes across in his conditional response. Both conditional statements conclude the protasis with Tipecha (8b, 8d). Tipecha rules its domain as the near subordinate of both Etnachta and Siluq, depending on where it occurs in the verse. The apodosis statements conclude as expected with Etnachta (8c) and Siluq (8e), which conforms to the pattern.

But half-verse conditionals often contain their own complexity. This example from Judges 14:13 illustrates how a stepped phrase can function within an apodosis. This verse begins in the middle of Samson's direct speech. Contextually, Judges 14:12b also contains a half-verse conditional that sets up this illustration. The conditional protasis in 13a begins with an אם particle and ends with the accent Segol. The apodosis in 13b begins with a *vav* conjunctive and concludes with the accent Etnachta. The presence of Zaqef in this clause forms a stepped phrase, since it ranks equally with Segol but exercises diminished influence in the same unit as Segol.[21] Zaqef continues to

---

[21] When Segol appears in a string of Zaqef clauses, Segol always substitutes for the first occurrence of Zaqef. Notice also that 13b contains a stepped "phrase" and not a stepped "clause." The entirety of 13b constitutes the clause.

function as a strong disjunctive, but its hierarchical role has been passed over due the stepping of phrases. Thus, Segol and Etnachta frame the conditional sentence according to the Masoretic pattern.[22]

Table 29. Pattern example: Judges 14:13

DS Protasis	וְאִם־לֹא תוּכְלוּ֙ לְהַגִּ֣יד לִ֔י ↘	13a
DS Apodosis	וּנְתַתֶּ֨ם אַתֶּ֥ם לִ֛י שְׁלֹשִׁ֥ים סְדִינִ֖ים	13b
(apodosis cont.)	וּשְׁלֹשִׁ֖ים חֲלִפֹ֥ות בְּגָדִֽים	--
Intro to DS	וַיֹּ֣אמְרוּ ל֔וֹ	13c
DS Response	ח֥וּדָה חִידָתְךָ֖	13d
DS Response	וְנִשְׁמָעֶֽנָּה׃	13e

At times the role of a stepped phrase will increase in syntactic significance despite its overall hierarchical diminishment. In the previous example the stepped phrase constituted a division within the apodosis. In the following example, the two conditionals will each use stepped phrasing differently. The first half-verse contains a stepped phrase which is the conditional protasis. The second half-verse divides within the apodosis using stepped phrasing, similar to Judges 14:13. The introduction to reported speech requires a significant disjunctive so that it remains distinct from the conditional statement. Yet, instead of nesting the conditional at a lower accent level, the Masoretes again use a stepped pattern.[23] Thus, 15a and 15b conclude with accents of the same

---

[22]Notice also that Etnachta in 13b occurs at the conclusion of direct speech and the transition of characters. See ch. 2 of this dissertation for this accent pattern.

[23]The first Zaqef has upgraded to Segol, as it commonly does in long verses

rank, but with very different functions. The Segol on 15a constitutes the strongest break of the half-verse and marks the boundary of direct speech. The conditional protasis begins in 15b and concludes with Zaqef; the apodosis begins in 15c and concludes with Etnachta, the governor of Zaqef. The Masoretes retain their pattern for conditional clauses despite the hierarchical diminishment of Zaqef in the overall Etnachta domain. In fact, by using the stepped phrases the Masoretes masterfully weave this accent pattern into a syntactically complex sentence.

Table 30. Pattern example: Judges 9:15

Intro to Quoted DS	וַיֹּ֤אמֶר הָאָטָד֙ אֶל־הָ֣עֵצִ֔ים	15a
DS Protasis #1	אִ֣ם בֶּאֱמֶ֗ת אַתֶּ֞ם מֹשְׁחִ֥ים אֹתִ֛י ↘	15b
(protasis cont.)	לְמֶ֖לֶךְ עֲלֵיכֶ֑ם	--
DS Apodosis #1	בֹּ֥אוּ חֲס֖וּ בְצִלִּ֑י	15c
DS Protasis #2	וְאִם־אַ֕יִן ↘	15d
DS Apodosis #2	תֵּצֵ֤א אֵשׁ֙ מִן־הָ֣אָטָ֔ד	15e
(apodosis cont.)	וְתֹאכַ֖ל אֶת־אַרְזֵ֥י הַלְּבָנֽוֹן׃	15f

---

with stepped Zaqefs. Jacobson calculates that half-verses using multiple stepped Zaqefs will upgrade the first Zaqef to Segol 80–90 percent of the time depending on the number of repetitions and number of words between Etnachta and Segol (*Chanting the Hebrew Bible: The Art of Cantillation*, 100). Wickes attributes this upgrade to musical variety. But he also notes that Segol tends to occur on the ninth word from Etnachta and beyond ("A Treatise on the Accentuation of the Twenty-One So-Called Prose Books of the Old Testament [טעמי כ״א ספרים]," in *Two Treatises on the Accentuation of the Old Testament*, ed. Harry M. Orlinsky [New York: KTAV, 1970], 72–73).

The second conditional clause (15d–f) does not need to account for an introductory statement. Therefore, the first Zaqef concludes the protasis (15d) and Siluq concludes the apodosis (15f). The intermediary Zaqef (15e) functions to mark a stepped phrase like the example from Judges 14:13 and should not be considered the conclusion of the apodosis. Thus, while the Masoretic pattern for conditional clauses may appear simple, complex syntax produces equally complex accent deployments.

4.4.3   COMPOUND CONDITIONAL SENTENCES.

The presence of multiple protases and apodoses creates another kind of complexity in conditional statements. Two of these compound patterns occur among the available passages from the book of Judges, each uniquely conforming to the overall Masoretic pattern for conditionals. First, Judges 9:19 exhibits one approach that groups multiple apodosis clauses together.[24]

Table 31. Pattern example: Judges 9:19

DS Protasis	וְאִם־בֶּאֱמֶת וּבְתָמִים עֲשִׂיתֶם	19a
(protasis cont.)	עִם־יְרֻבַּעַל וְעִם־בֵּיתוֹ הַיּוֹם הַזֶּה	--
DS Apodosis #1	שִׂמְחוּ בַּאֲבִימֶלֶךְ	19b
DS Apodosis #2	וְיִשְׂמַח גַּם־הוּא בָּכֶם׃	19c

The protasis concludes in 19a with Etnachta, Zaqef breaks the reciprocal apodoses in 19b, and the complete apodosis concludes in 19c with Sof

---

[24] For another clear example of this pattern see Jer 23:22.

Pasuq. Similar to Judges 9:15, these reciprocal apodoses need to be grouped closely together since they are not two independent apodoses. The Masoretes manage to both frame the verse according to their conditional accent pattern and to hold these latter clauses together as a unit.

The second example from Judges exhibits a slightly different approach to grouping multiple apodosis clauses. Whereas the Masoretes tightly grouped the resultant actions of Judges 9:19, they separate each apodosis out in Judges 13:23. This is also the first example of an "unreal" conditional (לוּ), whereas all previous examples have used "real" conditionals (אִם). Structurally, real and unreal conditionals operate in the same manner, as do their accents.

Table 32. Pattern example: Judges 13:23

Intro to DS	וַתֹּאמֶר לוֹ אִשְׁתּוֹ	23a
DS Protasis [Pashta]	לוּ חָפֵץ יְהוָה לַהֲמִיתֵנוּ	23b
DS Apodosis #1 [Zaqef]	לֹא־לָקַח מִיָּדֵנוּ עֹלָה וּמִנְחָה	23c
Apodosis #2 [Etnachta]	וְלֹא הֶרְאָנוּ אֶת־כָּל־אֵלֶּה	23d
Apodosis #3 [Sof Pasuq]	וְכָעֵת לֹא הִשְׁמִיעָנוּ כָּזֹאת׃	23e

After a brief introductory statement, the protasis concludes on the level four accent Pashta (23b). The first apodosis statement concludes with the level three accent Zaqef, lord of Pashta (23c). The second apodosis statement concludes with the level two accent Etnachta, lord of Zaqef (23d). The third apodosis statement concludes with the level one accent Sof Pasuq, lord of Etnachta (23e). This is one of the classic Masoretic ways of accenting a list, with the accent getting stronger towards the end in order to keep all components together.²⁵ Thus, the conditional properly concludes in 23c, then adds another conclusion in 23d, and another in 23e. While this may appear to take liberties with the Masoretic pattern, in actuality it binds together two Masoretic patterns—conditionals and lists. So, awareness of the typical Masoretic pattern actually serves to clarify the interpretation of this verse rather than to create confusion.

4.4.4   PARTIAL-VERSE CONDITIONAL SENTENCES.

Judges 13:23 illustrated how the Masoretes weave multiple patterns together in the midst of a compound conditional. Judges 13:16 exhibits this complexity with multiple conditional statements compounded by a subordinate clause that is not part of the direct speech. Chapter 2 outlined how the Masoretes tend to use Etnachta to conclude mid-verse direct speech.²⁶ That pattern takes priority in this verse (16e), thus all other accents adjust to this predominant pattern. But such adjustment does not mean the Masoretes abandon all other patterns. Here they manage to frame two conditional clauses within the first half-verse. They frame the first conditional with Pashta and Zaqef, the second with Zaqef and Etnachta.

---

²⁵See also Exod 12:29, Deut 7:1, and Dan 3:2, 5 for examples of lists with the accents growing stronger on each item.

²⁶The logical break for Etnachta would come at the end of 16c. This would provide balance with regard to verse length and neatly separate the two conditional clauses. However, this logical break would create confusion in 16e as to the conclusion of direct speech. The reader might naturally conclude that 16f continues the direct speech on to the end of the verse. Since a third person entity was introduced in 16e, the third person verb in 16f could easily be mistaken as referring to that entity. Thus, the Masoretes have to make use of their pattern for concluding direct speech, and yet still frame the multiple conditional clauses. See ch. 2 of this dissertation for more specifics on the direct speech pattern.

Table 33. Pattern example: Judges 13:16

Intro to DS	וַיֹּ֩אמֶר֩ מַלְאַ֨ךְ יְהוָ֜ה אֶל־מָנ֗וֹחַ	16a
DS Protasis #1	אִם־תַּעְצְרֵ֙נִי֙ ↙	16b
DS Apodosis #1	לֹא־אֹכַ֣ל בְּלַחְמֶ֔ךָ	16c
DS Protasis #2	וְאִם־תַּעֲשֶׂ֣ה עֹלָ֔ה ↙	16d
DS Apodosis #2	לַיהוָ֖ה תַּעֲלֶ֑נָּה	16e
Subordinate Clause	כִּ֚י לֹא־יָדַ֣ע מָנ֔וֹחַ כִּֽי־מַלְאַ֥ךְ יְהוָ֖ה הֽוּא׃	16f

The first protasis (16b) is a stepped phrase relative to the introduction to direct speech (16a). The second protasis (16d) is a stepped phrase relative to the first conditional (16b–c). Once again the Masoretes masterfully weave their patterns together in order to signal multiple dimensions of syntax in one verse.

4.4.5 MULTIPLE-VERSE CONDITIONAL SENTENCES.

If partial-verse conditionals require weaving together multiple syntactic features, then multi-verse conditionals expand that challenge to even greater lengths. Judges 11:30–31 represents a short example.[27] The protasis concludes on the Sof Pasuq of 30c, the highest possible rank. In order to follow the Masoretic pattern the apodosis must conclude with an accent one rank higher. In this case there are no higher rank accents, so the expected conclusion to the apodosis must also be Sof Pasuq. The apodosis begins in 31a, only to be temporally qualified in 31b, then

---

[27]The curved downward arrow indicates clause subordination. The straight downward arrow indicates resumption after a temporal interjection.

resumes and concludes in 31c. Thus, both the protasis and apodosis conclude on the same accent because the second accent could not outrank the first.

Table 34. Pattern example: Judges 11:30–31

Intro to DS	וַיִּדַּ֨ר יִפְתָּ֥ח נֶ֛דֶר לַיהוָ֖ה	30a
Intro to DS	וַיֹּאמַ֑ר	30b
DS Protasis	אִם־נָת֥וֹן תִּתֵּ֛ן אֶת־בְּנֵ֥י עַמּ֖וֹן בְּיָדִֽי׃ ↘	30c
DS Apodosis	וְהָיָ֣ה הַיּוֹצֵ֗א אֲשֶׁ֨ר יֵצֵ֜א מִדַּלְתֵ֤י בֵיתִי֙ לִקְרָאתִ֔י	31a
DS Temporal	↧ בְּשׁוּבִ֥י בְשָׁל֖וֹם מִבְּנֵ֣י עַמּ֑וֹן	31b
DS Apodosis	וְהָיָה֙ לַֽיהוָ֔ה וְהַעֲלִיתִ֖הוּ עוֹלָֽה׃	31c

A further example from outside the book of Judges shows this complexity across the span of three verses. The dividing line for the protasis and apodosis occurs right in the middle of the middle verse. In Genesis 28:20–22 the conditional protasis begins in 20b and crosses over to 21a. The conditional apodosis begins in 21b and crosses over to 22b.[28] Thus, both parts of the conditional expand beyond the constraints of verse boundaries. Yet, even with such expansion of the protasis and apodosis, the overall Masoretic pattern remains intact. The protasis concludes on 21a with Etnachta and the apodosis concludes on 22b with

---

[28]One might argue that the apodosis properly concludes in Gen 28:21b and does not cross a verse boundary. While it is possible that v. 22 only contains related results and not the direct consequence of vv. 20–21, this seems unlikely. The nominal form of the clauses in v. 22, with a constituent placed in front of the verb, makes these perfect candidates for continuation of the apodosis begun in v. 21b. But in both interpretations, the apodosis concludes with Siluq according to the pattern.

Sof Pasuq. So, despite the syntactical complexities that extend across multiple verses, the Masoretes manage to frame the unit according to the same pattern they use for all other conditionals.

Table 35. Pattern example: Genesis 28:20–22

Intro to DS	וַיִּדַּ֥ר יַעֲקֹ֖ב נֶ֣דֶר לֵאמֹ֑ר	20a
Protasis begins:	אִם־יִהְיֶ֨ה אֱלֹהִ֜ים עִמָּדִ֗י	20b
(conditions)	וּשְׁמָרַ֙נִי֙ בַּדֶּ֤רֶךְ הַזֶּה֙ אֲשֶׁ֣ר אָנֹכִ֣י הוֹלֵ֔ךְ	20c
(conditions)	וְנָֽתַן־לִ֥י לֶ֛חֶם לֶאֱכֹ֖ל וּבֶ֥גֶד לִלְבֹּֽשׁ׃	20d
(conditions)	וְשַׁבְתִּ֥י בְשָׁל֖וֹם אֶל־בֵּ֣ית אָבִ֑י	21a
Apodosis Begins:	וְהָיָ֧ה יְהוָ֛ה לִ֖י לֵאלֹהִֽים׃	21b
(conclusions)	וְהָאֶ֣בֶן הַזֹּ֗את אֲשֶׁר־שַׂ֙מְתִּי֙ מַצֵּבָ֔ה	22a
	יִהְיֶ֖ה בֵּ֣ית אֱלֹהִ֑ים	--
(conclusions)	וְכֹל֙ אֲשֶׁ֣ר תִּתֶּן־לִ֔י עַשֵּׂ֖ר אֲעַשְּׂרֶ֥נּוּ לָֽךְ׃	22b

The Masoretic pattern for framing conditionals occurs at all levels of the text: full-verse (Judg 6:17; cf. Gen 18:3), half-verse (Judg 4:8; 14:13; 9:15), compound protasis/apodosis (9:19–20; 13:23), partial-verse (Judg 13:16), and multi-verse (Judg 11:30–31; Gen 28:20–22). At times the pattern appears simple; at others the Masoretes weave it into a complex syntactical construction. Regardless, the Masoretes frame conditional statements with accents of different ranks; the subordinate rank concludes the protasis, the superior rank concludes the apodosis.

4.5 DIVERGENCE FROM THE PATTERN

Notable exceptions to the Masoretic pattern exist within the book of Judges and throughout the Hebrew Bible. These divergent examples demand an examination despite being vastly outnumbered. But, in the end, such divergent examples actually prove the pattern. When the Masoretes diverge from their typical pattern for discernible reasons, the divergence solidifies the intentionality of the pattern. Such is the case with the divergent examples from Judges. Each of these passages exhibit signs of intentional choices by the Masoretes to go against their typical pattern for conditional clauses. In addition, this unit will discuss the major textual variant example from Judges 16:13 and two passages that E. J. Revell raises as problematic for the accent system in general.

4.5.1 DIVERGENT EXAMPLES IN JUDGES

Multi-verse conditionals struggle with clarity regarding the boundaries of the protasis and apodosis. Gideon's hesitancy in the face of battle illustrates this problem (Judg 6:36–37). He begins his request with a conditional (36b–c), offers an interjection (37a), then proceeds into a second compound conditional (37b–c). This accumulation of clauses finally lands on the apodosis (37d). The second conditional statement resolves without much trouble. Its protasis begins in the second half-verse (37b) and includes a contrast relationship with the next clause (37c). These two clauses make up the conditional protasis (37b–c). Zaqef rules over the protasis with Revia dividing the contrasting statements. The apodosis concludes in 37e with Siluq, the expected lord of Zaqef. Thus, this second conditional perfectly fits the Masoretic pattern for conditionals in a half-verse.

Table 36. Divergence example: Judges 6:36–37

Intro to DS	וַיֹּ֤אמֶר גִּדְעוֹן֙ אֶל־הָ֣אֱלֹהִ֔ים	36a
DS Protasis	אִם־יֶשְׁךָ֞ מוֹשִׁ֧יעַ בְּיָדִ֛י אֶת־יִשְׂרָאֵ֖ל ↙	36b
DS Comparative Clause	כַּאֲשֶׁ֥ר דִּבַּֽרְתָּ׃	36c
DS Interjection	הִנֵּ֣ה אָנֹכִ֗י מַצִּ֛יג אֶת־גִּזַּ֥ת הַצֶּ֖מֶר בַּגֹּ֑רֶן	37a
DS Protasis	אִ֡ם טַל֩ יִהְיֶ֨ה עַֽל־הַגִּזָּ֜ה לְבַדָּ֗הּ ↙	37b
DS Contrast Phrase	וְעַל־כָּל־הָאָ֣רֶץ חֹ֔רֶב	37c
DS Apodosis	וְיָ֣דַעְתִּ֔י כִּֽי־תוֹשִׁ֥יעַ בְּיָדִ֖י אֶת־יִשְׂרָאֵ֑ל	37d
DS Comparative Clause	כַּאֲשֶׁ֥ר דִּבַּֽרְתָּ׃	37e

But the conditional statement of 37b–e only forms part of Gideon's overall statement. The first conditional statement constitutes the overall desire of Gideon. In other words, Gideon only cares about the dampness of the fleece (37b) because it reflects on God's intentions to save Israel by his hand (36b). The first conditional protasis concludes in 36c with Sof Pasuq; the interjection that stands in place of an apodosis concludes in 37a with Etnachta. But this "apodosis" is not complete and should not be considered a true apodosis. Rather, this statement serves as a bridge to the second conditional statement. Gideon's response to God could be summarized like this, "If you will save Israel by me, then I need some proof: if you show me this sign, then I will know that you will save Israel by me." The apodosis to the initial conditional exists in two stages: (1) an interjection that bridges to a second conditional, and (2) a second conditional sentence that serves to complete the first conditional clause. Thus, the initial protasis

CHAPTER 4: ACCENTS FRAMING CONDITIONAL SENTENCES   99

concludes with Sof Pasuq and the ultimate apodosis concludes with Sof Pasuq, the same pattern as in other multi-verse conditionals. The Masoretes have marked one half-verse compound conditional according to their pattern (37b–e) and yet still frame the entire conditional in a sensible manner.

Such exceptional constructions sometimes call for exceptional choices, as with Judges 6:36–37. And emphatic verses call for emphatic markers, as with Judges 9:20. Earlier Judges 9:19 presented an example of a compound apodosis. But this subsequent verse marks the pinnacle of an emotional speech. Whereas 9:19 expressed the potential, though unlikely, results of the unholy alliance between Avimelekh and the lords of Shekhem, 9:20 expresses a wish for judgment on their pact.

Table 37. Divergence example: Judges 9:20

DS Protasis [contrast]	וְאִם־אַ֕יִן ↘	20a
DS Apodosis #1a—action	תֵּצֵ֤א אֵשׁ֙ מֵאֲבִימֶ֔לֶךְ	20b
Apodosis #1b—result	וְתֹאכַ֛ל אֶת־בַּעֲלֵ֥י שְׁכֶ֖ם וְאֶת־בֵּ֣ית מִלּ֑וֹא	20c
DS Apodosis #2a—action	וְתֵצֵ֨א אֵ֜שׁ מִבַּעֲלֵ֤י שְׁכֶם֙ וּמִבֵּ֣ית מִלּ֔וֹא	20d
Apodosis #2b—result	וְתֹאכַ֖ל אֶת־אֲבִימֶֽלֶךְ׃	20e

Each of these two apodoses consist of two parts, an action and a result. Both imperfect verbs are in the jussive mood describing a wish or desired outcome. In this case the verbs יצא and אכל must be read together expressing a single wish. Thus, the protasis concludes in 20a, and the first apodosis concludes in 20c. The second apodosis flips the recipient of the action so that the overall results are reciprocal. The second apodosis concludes in 20e.

The Masoretes could have mirrored the accent pattern of Judges 9:19, dividing the two apodoses on a lower accent level, but ultimately grouping them together with the major disjunction (see table 31). This would have required them to place Etnachta on אִי in 20a. While it is possible for Etnachta to occur on the first word of a verse, this formation is rare in the Bible.[29] Instead they have created a typical conditional statement from the protasis in 20a through the first apodosis in 20b–c. The introduction of Etnachta at this point makes logical sense, but it also splits the apodoses. Etnachta will commonly split a pair, especially if the pair demands attention as a significant part of the verse.[30] Thus, at the emotional climax of Yotam's parable, Etnachta strikes the heart of the verse. Such a semantic use does not contravene Masoretic conventions, rather its divergence from the usual pattern signals the high water mark of the declaration.

One final divergent passage from the book of Judges appears very similar to the multiple-apodosis example from Judges 13:23. This verse also contains multiple apodoses, but their accent configuration differs. In Judges 13:23, the protasis concluded with a level four disjunctive, Pashta (see table 32). The first apodosis concluded a complete conditional statement (Zaqef), each subsequent apodosis adding on another conclusion after the manner of a list (Etnachta, Siluq/Sof Pasuq). Here in Judges 21:21, the accent development is not quite as simple (i.e., the apodoses do not form a list with ascending accents).

---

[29]Etnachta occurs on the first Masoretic word of a verse 31 times out of 21,567 occurrences of Etnachta in the entire Hebrew Bible. For example, Ezek 23:2 parallels Judg 9:20 in that the first word is actually two words joined by Maqef. If the Masoretes separated these words, and Etnachta landed on the second, this would fit another rare paradigm that occurs only 68 times. Thus, while the Masoretes do place Etnachta very far forward, they rarely do so.

[30]Fuller and Choi, *Biblical Hebrew Syntax*, Accents §9.C.2.a.

While the apodoses exhibit the same progression—Zaqef, Etnachta, Siluq/Sof Pasuq—the accent concluding the protasis changes the scenario.

The protasis concludes on Segol (21b), which makes the first apodosis a stepped phrase (21c), not the conclusion of the apodosis. The conditional concludes in 21d with Etnachta, thus tightly binding the first two apodoses together (21c, d). The clause in 21e adds a subsequent apodosis to the initial conclusion, much like the list of Judges 13:23. This structure actually makes good sense of the text. The commands "to come out" (יצא) and "to snatch" (חטף) form a singular action (21c, d). Whereas the final command, "to go" (הלך), constitutes a separate action. In other words, while three verbs make up the conclusion to this conditional, the Masoretes have framed it so that readers see two main actions—the taking of the women (21c, d) and the fleeing to a distant region (21e). They have used the accents to help readers properly group the clauses and, as a result, better understand their relationship.

Table 38. Divergence example: Judges 21:21

Imperatives	וּרְאִיתֶ֗ם וְהִנֵּ֞ה	21a
Protasis [Segol]	אִם־יֵצְא֨וּ בְנוֹת־שִׁיל֥וֹ לָח֖וּל בַּמְּחֹל֑וֹת	21b
Apodosis #1 [Zaqef] (1a)	וִֽיצָאתֶם֙ מִן־הַכְּרָמִ֔ים	21c
Apodosis #2 [Etnachta] (1b)	וַחֲטַפְתֶּ֥ם לָכֶ֛ם אִ֥ישׁ אִשְׁתּ֖וֹ מִבְּנ֣וֹת שִׁיל֑וֹ	21d
Apodosis #3 [Siluq] (2)	וַהֲלַכְתֶּ֖ם אֶ֥רֶץ בִּנְיָמִֽן׃	21e

The divergent passages from the book of Judges exhibit truly exceptional grammatical constructions (Judg 6:36–37), emphatic structures (Judg 9:20), and very precise parsing of the clauses (Judg

21:21). In each of these cases, the Masoretes have generally maintained their pattern for framing conditional sentences, yet they also account for the complexity of these verses. Approaching these examples with a general framework for how the Masoretes accent a conditional statement allows the interpreter to more clearly discern the meaning. In some cases the Masoretes merely clarify the reading (6:36–37; 21:21), in others they signal elements of emphasis and literary interest (9:20).

4.5.2 TEXT-CRITICAL ISSUE IN JUDGES

Block summarizes the opinion of many regarding the textual character of the book of Judges: "Compared to the rest of the historiographic writings of the Old Testament, the Hebrew text of Judges preserved in the Leningrad Codex of AD 1008 ... and the Aleppo Codex from the early tenth century AD is relatively pure.... The instances in which the MT can be improved upon by appealing to the LXX are relatively few."[31] Nevertheless, Judges 16:13 qualifies as one of those "few" text-critical issues due to three factors: (1) the incomplete conditional in 13g, (2) the complete conditionals for the three other tests by Delilah (16:7, 11, 17),[32] and (3) the incomplete transition beginning 16:14. I understand the longer reading of LXX-B to be closest to the original,

---

[31] Daniel I. Block, *Judges, Ruth,* NAC 6 (Nashville: B&H, 1999), 72. Marcos concurs with this statement: "The Masoretic text of Judges in its final form is a text relatively well preserved except for ch. 5. Most of M's readings should be preferred over the variant readings of the versions or a good number of conjectures suggested by previous editors and commentators" (*Judges,* Biblia Hebraica Quinta 7 [Stuttgart: Deutsche Bibelgesellschaft, 2011], 7*).

[32] The first two responses by Samson appear as full-verse conditionals (Judg 16:7, 11). The final response by Samson appears as a half-verse conditional (Judg 6:17). If the text in Judg 6:13 appeared as a complete conditional (protasis + apodosis), it too would be accented as a half-verse conditional, similar to 6:17.

and the MT, though perhaps the more difficult reading, contains an inadvertently shortened reading.³³

Table 39. Text-critical example: Judges 16:13

Intro to DS	וַתֹּאמֶר דְּלִילָה אֶל־שִׁמְשׁוֹן	13a
DS Accusation #1	עַד־הֵנָּה הֵתַלְתָּ בִּי	13b
DS Accusation #2	וַתְּדַבֵּר אֵלַי כְּזָבִים	13c
DS Request	הַגִּידָה לִּי	13d
DS Content	בַּמֶּה תֵּאָסֵר	13e
Intro to DS	וַיֹּאמֶר אֵלֶיהָ	13f
DS Protasis	↙ אִם־תַּאַרְגִי אֶת־שֶׁבַע מַחְלְפוֹת רֹאשִׁי	13g
	עִם־הַמַּסָּכֶת:	--

The text of LXX Vaticanus offers the closest reading to what the original Hebrew may have said.³⁴ The scribe likely made a simple error of haplography which jumped from one occurrence of the word המסכת

---

³³See appendix 2 for a complete discussion and comparative table of the various ancient language renderings.

³⁴Marcos writes that "the most ancient text attainable for the Greek translation of Judges is a relatively free translation compared with the text of *Vaticanus* and not exempt from revisions. Consequently, it cannot be described typologically as reflecting a 'shorter text' than the Masoretic one. Moreover, *it can be asserted that the Hebrew text known by the Greek translator of Judges was one only slightly different from the Masoretic text*" ("The Hebrew and Greek Texts of Judges," in *The Earliest Text of the Hebrew Bible: The Relationship between the Masoretic Text and the Hebrew Base of the Septuagint Reconsidered*, ed. Adrian Schenker [Atlanta: Society of Biblical Literature, 2003], 15 [emphasis added]).

to the next.[35] If the Masoretes had possessed the complete conditional at the end of verse 13, their accentuation scheme would have differed only slightly. Whether or not a text-critical explanation best accounts for the condition of this verse, the question of the accents remains the central concern in this dissertation. Because the conditional in Judges 16:13 remains incomplete in the Masoretic text, this example should not be counted as a true divergence from the pattern for conditional statements

4.5.3 OBJECTIONS TO THE MASORETIC SYSTEM FROM OUTSIDE JUDGES

Divergent examples rise from across the biblical landscape, but challenging passages only confirm the intentional nature of this Masoretic pattern. E. J. Revell raises two such examples which possess a different character from those already examined. Revell has provided numerous significant works related to Masoretic studies, one focused exclusively on the pausal system. While he does not aim to bring this feature of the text into conflict with the accents, his study uncovers some challenging examples. Such examples lead Revell to conclude,

> Not only must the common view, that pausal forms are dependent on the major disjunctive accents, be rejected, it must also be accepted that the received accentuation of the text often does not represent the arrangement of words which gave rise to the received vocalization.... *Inconsistency between vocalization and accentuation is so common in the text (as will be shown below), that it must be held to be characteristic of it.* The view that accentuation and voweling do not derive from the same tradition cannot be avoided.[36]

---

[35]Barthélemy labels this "un cas très typique d'homéotéleuton" and cites Codex B as the best reading (*Critique Textuelle de l'Ancien Testament*, vol. 1 [Fribourg, Switzerland: Éditions Universitaires Fribourg/Suisse, 1982], 112).

[36]E. J. Revell, *The Pausal System: Divisions in the Hebrew Biblical Text as Marked By Voweling and Stress Position,* ed. Raymond de Hoop and Paul Sanders (Sheffield: Sheffield Phoenix, 2015), 3 (emphasis added).

His conclusion that voweling and accentuation represent two independent systems comes from these examples of "common inconsistency."[37] But it remains to be seen whether these examples are actual inconsistencies between the two systems, or whether they exhibit traits of intentional divergence.

Malachi 1:6 includes two short conditional statements which diverge from the accent framing pattern. Instead of the expected disjunctive on the protasis followed by a disjunctive of a superior rank on the apodosis, this verse employs conjunctive accents on the protasis followed by level five accents on the apodoses. This verse exhibits such a full range of accents because the Masoretes placed Etnachta so early in a rather lengthy verse. The Masoretes use Etnachta within the main body of direct speech to divide the indicative statements from the conditional questions. And these conditionals, as Revell points out, use the pausal system to mark the end of the protasis.[38] This use of the

---

[37] Revell also understands that the voweling was "fixed" in the text before the accents; by "fixed" he means, in the oral tradition (*Nesiga (Retraction of Word Stress) in Tiberian Hebrew* [Madrid: Instituto de Filologia, C.S.I.C., 1987], §1.15). Dotan posits that the accents were written down first because the nuance of accentuation was more likely to be lost in the oral tradition ("Masorah," in vol. 13 of *Encyclopedia Judaica* [New York: Macmillan Reference, 2007], 603–56 at 627). Revell recognizes Dotan's study but maintains that it refers only to the introduction of the symbols into the written text, not which system was first fixed in the oral tradition. So, while Revell sees potential for the vocalization tradition extending back to the time of Ezra, he understands the accents as a later musical development for textual recitation (*The Pausal System*, 7; see also Geoffrey Khan, *A Short Introduction to the Tiberian Masoretic Bible and Its Reading Tradition,* ed. George Anton Kiraz [Piscataway, NJ: Gorgias, 2012], 61). But if the accents correspond to Hebrew syntax, and not merely a pattern of recitation, then likely this system also extends back to Ezra and his scribes (*Short Introduction*, 38).

[38] Revell points to examples in Num 35:16, 17, 18; 1 Kgs 20:18; Hab 2:3 for the typical pattern of pausal forms on conditionals. Each of these examples exhibit the typical accent pattern for conditional statements described in this chapter. This makes Mal 1:6 even more intriguing as a divergent example.

pausal system with a conjunctive accent on a protasis clause diverges from the pattern for conditional statements.

Both protasis clauses conclude on the word אני with the pausal Qamats, instead of the typical Chatef-Patach. The first אני also displays stress retraction due to the pausal form with munach standing below the first syllable. The second אני appears to resist stress retraction because Telishah Qetanah is a post-positive accent.[39]

Table 40. Divergence example: Malachi 1:6

DS Indicative Statement #1	בֵּן יְכַבֵּד אָב	6a
DS Indicative Statement #2	וְעֶבֶד אֲדֹנָיו	6b
DS Protasis #1	וְאִם־אָב אָנִי	6c
DS Apodosis #1	אַיֵּה כְבוֹדִי	6d
DS Protasis #2	וְאִם־אֲדוֹנִים אָנִי	6e
DS Apodosis #2	אַיֵּה מוֹרָאִי	6f
Conclusion to DS	אָמַר ׀ יְהוָה צְבָאוֹת לָכֶם הַכֹּהֲנִים בּוֹזֵי שְׁמִי	6g
Intro to DS	וַאֲמַרְתֶּם	6h
DS Question	בַּמֶּה בָזִינוּ אֶת־שְׁמֶךָ׃	6i

In actuality the accent has shifted with the pausal form, and some modern versions of the Hebrew Bible even mark this shift by doubling the accent symbol.[40] This retraction of word stress serves to slow down

---

[39]Both lengthening of the vowel and a change in syllabic stress are common for pausal forms. Jacobson, *Chanting the Hebrew Bible: The Art of Cantillation*, 39.

[40]Jacobson, *Chanting the Hebrew Bible: The Art of Cantillation*, 135.

the reading without the use of a disjunctive accent.⁴¹ If we understand the typical Masoretic pattern for conditional clauses, this seems like a very reasonable compromise. Since level five accents are the lowest rank of disjunctives, and these occur on the apodosis, there exists no level six disjunctives for the protasis. Instead the Masoretes use pausal vowels with conjunctive accents to create a slight pause at the end of the protasis.⁴² They therefore maintain their pattern for conditional clauses by improvising a solution for low level accentuation.⁴³

Perhaps an even more difficult divergence arises in Genesis 13:9. Here two conditionals stand back to back, one conforming to the typical accentuation pattern and one diverging from the pattern. The Masoretic use of Maqef here creates statements made up of only one word for each half of the conditional.⁴⁴ The divergence occurs in 9c where a reader might expect Pashta to conclude the protasis, were this marked strictly according to the prevailing pattern. Instead, Munach joins the protasis to the apodosis.

---

⁴¹By contrast, Maqef is "a device that speeds up the sluggish rhythm created by too many accented syllables" (Jacobson, *Chanting the Hebrew Bible: The Art of Cantillation*, 329).

⁴²Compare also the Masoretic use of Paseq to introduce a slight pause with conjunctive accents. See William Wickes, "A Treatise on the Accentuation of the Twenty-One So-Called Prose Books of the Old Testament (טעמי כ״א ספרים)," in *Two Treatises on the Accentuation of the Old Testament,* ed. Harry M. Orlinsky (New York: KTAV, 1970), 122–24.

⁴³My recognition that the Masoretes maintain their accentuation pattern does not draw any conclusions about the historical development of these two systems. While this provides one piece of evidence that supports the position that these two systems have always existed side by side, such a conclusion is not necessary. It remains sufficient to see that the Masoretes have used a feature outside the accents in order to maintain their typical accentuation pattern for conditional statements.

⁴⁴Dresher calls this phenomenon "simplification" which the Masoretes use to speed up the speech ("The Prosodic Basis of the Tiberian System of Hebrew Accents," *Language* 70 [March 1994]: 36). This is similar to Jacobson's appraisal of Maqef.

Table 41. Divergence example: Genesis 13:9

DS Question	הֲלֹא כָל־הָאָרֶץ לְפָנֶיךָ	9a
DS Imperative	הִפָּרֶד נָא מֵעָלָי	9b
DS Protasis #1	↘ אִם־הַשְּׂמֹאל	9c
DS Apodosis #1	וְאֵימִנָה	9d
DS Protasis #2	↘ וְאִם־הַיָּמִין	9e
DS Apodosis #2	וְאַשְׂמְאִילָה׃	9f

Three observations help to categorize this example: (1) the clauses are short, as already mentioned; (2) the clauses are lexically marked with אם and *vav*; (3) the clauses together constitute what appears to be a common saying. Addressing the third observation, nothing in the context of Genesis 13 indicates that שמאל or ימין indicate specific geographic directions. In fact, Abram's statement in 9a seems to indicate that these two men were surveying the entirety of the land around them. Abram's conditional statements use שמאל and ימין as a means of invoking a contrast. In other words, "whichever way you choose, Lot, I will go the opposite." When Lot chooses the lands of the Jordan valley, and ultimately the east side of the Dead Sea, Abram stays in the land of Canaan on the west side of the river. Thus, Abram's words prove to be a statement of contrast and not intended to denote any specific geographic location.

The second observation, that these conditionals exhibit clear lexical boundaries, also factors into the puzzle of Genesis 13:9. Understanding both sets of conditionals as a united statement of contrast makes good sense of the accents. Both conditionals reside in the second half of the verse, after Etnachta. This keeps the ideas closer together instead of separating them (cf. Judg 9:15 where two alternative conditionals are split by Etnachta). Within this united set of clauses, a *vav* conjunctive serves to both connect ideas ("but," 9e) but also to complete the conditionals ("then," 9d, f). Thus, these conditionals exhibit the clear lexical boundaries of אם and *vav* not present in all conditional statements.

No semantic issues appear to influence the divergence of the first conditional. At this point two alternative explanations might offer some help: (1) pragmatic observations, and (2) accent rules. Pragmatically speaking, it appears that in this case the Masoretic reading tradition reads the first alternative more quickly than the second, with the biggest break still remaining between the conditionals. In other words, the reading slows down in the second conditional as Abram's direct speech draws to a close. Dresher would likely point to this verse as an example of the prosodic basis for the Masoretic accents.[45] Similarly, Janis would likely point to this verse as an example of the recitation style of the Hebrew.[46] In one sense they would both be correct. Pragmatically, the accents in this verse appear to conform to a pattern of speech or recitation.

But the first of the three initial observations proves the be the key that unlocks this mystery—the shortness of the clauses, and more precisely, the words. The pattern for conditionals in this chapter requires the protasis to conclude with a subordinate accent, the apodosis with the superior accent. In this case, though we expect Pashta to conclude

---

[45] Bezalel Elan Dresher, "Biblical Accents: Prosody" (Boston: Brill, 2013), 295.

[46] Norman Janis, "A Grammar of the Biblical Accents" (PhD diss., Harvard University, 1987), 59.

protasis #1, Pashta cannot be used. "It is only when Zaqeph's word is *long*, that the foretone Pashṭa appears; otherwise, the servus (Munach) is employed."[47] By "long word" Wickes means that the word with Zaqef has two or more vowels before the tone syllable, or one long vowel followed by Meteg or Sheva.[48] In this case, וְאֵימָ֫נָה from line 9d has only one vowel before the tone syllable and, though the vowel is long, the Tsere-Yod is not followed by a Meteg or Sheva.[49] So, while this example exhibits some interesting pragmatic features, ultimately it breaks the pattern for framing conditionals due to a technicality of accentuation.

4.6 CONCLUSION

The Masoretes frame conditional sentences with disjunctive accents that increase one level from the protasis to the apodosis. The protasis receives the subordinate accent, the apodosis its superior accent. This pattern occurs in 90 percent of examples from from the book of Judges, whether the verse contains a full-verse, half-verse, partial-verse, multi-verse, or compound conditional. The few examples that diverge from this pattern also show a general conformity to the pattern but make slight adjustments due to the complexity of the syntax (Judg 6:36–37; 9:20: 21:21). Additionally, these divergent examples in Judges indicate that the Masoretic intentionally frame conditional sentences.

---

[47]Wickes, "Accentuation of the Twenty-One Prose Books," 75. Wickes contrasts Gen 21:24 with 15:3 where the differing lengths of Abraham's name alters the accent on the preceding verb. He provides numerous other such contrasts and describes it as a musical principle.

[48]Wickes, "Accentuation of the Twenty-One Prose Books," 62.

[49]Consonants with Sheva never constitute a syllable because they are not full vowels (Russell T. Fuller and Kyoungwon Choi, *Invitation to Biblical Hebrew: A Beginning Grammar* [Grand Rapids: Kregel Academic, 2006], §3.4).

Two other examples outside the book of Judges pose a different set of challenges to this proposal. Malachi 1:6 demonstrates how the Masoretes handle conditionals at the lowest level of the accent hierarchy. Their solution uses pausal forms for the protasis and level five disjunctives for the apodosis, thus maintaining their pattern. Genesis 13:9 provides an exceptional example where the finer nature of the accent rules overturns the accent pattern. Nevertheless, the choices of the Masoretes in both of these cases make better sense in light of their general pattern for framing conditionals.

The high frequency of this pattern in the book of Judges indicates that it constitutes a priority pattern for the Masoretes. Such regularity also makes it predictable; and predictability makes this pattern useful to readers. While readers may often discern the bounds of a conditional statement based on the presence of אם and *vav*, such lexical markers are not always present. And even when present, the conditional may conclude before the end of the verse. The Masoretic pattern of framing conditionals confirms the suppositions of readers in more obvious passages and guides readers through more difficult passages.

CHAPTER 5
ACCENTS AT CONTRAST STRUCTURES

5.1   INTRODUCTION

The foregoing studies have examined literary and lexical features of the Hebrew text. While the context helps the reader discern the conclusion of direct speech, the accents also prove a useful guide in avoiding any ambiguity. The interjection ועתה asserts itself prominently, and the accents parallel the force of this lexical marker. The two-step rhythm of conditional statements reflects in the framing pattern used by the Masoretes. The next textual landmark introduces a new set of challenges. Due to lexical and syntactic mismatches between languages, difficulties arise in discerning contrast relationships in the absence of an explicit contrastive particle. In places where a translation language may require a contrast particle, the ever-present Hebrew *vav* appears. This chapter will examine how the accents help readers distinguish contexts of contrast in biblical Hebrew prose texts.

5.2   GRAMMATICAL CONSIDERATIONS

The major lexicons divide the roles of *vav* up into numerous categories: conjunction, emphasis, explanation, alternative, and adversative (to name a few).[1] Brown, Driver, and Briggs comment, "[*vav*] is used very freely and widely in Hebrew, but also with much delicacy, to express

---

[1] See especially Ludwig Koehler and Walter Baumgartner, "ו," in *The Hebrew and Aramaic Lexicon of the Old Testament*, electronic ed., trans. M. E. J. Richardson (Altamonte Springs, FL: OakTree Software, 2000).

relations and shades of meaning which Western languages would usually indicate by distinct particles."² Hebrew also has distinct particles that function in multiple ways: רַק ,אַךְ ,אֲבָל ,אֶפֶס כִּי ,אוּלָם ,כִּי ,כִּי אִם. But these particles occur sparingly. The far more prevalent conjunction remains the letter *vav*.

It may be most advantageous to begin with a default view of *vav* as a simple conjoining letter, the nature of that conjunction to be determined by the context.³ Steiner writes, "Much of the ambiguity that has been attributed to ו- actually resides elsewhere in the sentence, sometimes elsewhere in its surface structure and sometimes elsewhere in its underlying structure."⁴ He goes on to conclude that the most explicit structural signal for contrast comes through the word order.⁵ So, while Hebrew contrast structures hinge around numerous particles, the key to discerning the contrastive sense of *vav* lies more in the surrounding context than the conjunction itself.⁶

---

²Francis Brown, Samuel R. Driver, and Charles A. Briggs, *The Brown-Driver-Briggs Hebrew and English Lexicon* (Peabody, MA: Hendrickson, 2012), 252.

³English clearly represents a language that prefers distinct particles to indicate contrast. While "*but* is often described as logically equivalent to *and* .... *But* clearly means more than [*and*], and this 'more' is generally said to be contrast of some sort." These contrasts can be defined as (1) a denial of the expected phrase, or (2) a real semantic contrast, items that are polar opposites (Marianne Celce-Murcia and Diane Larsen-Freeman, *The Grammar Book: An ESL/EFL Teacher's Course* [Boston: Heinle-Cengage Learning, 1999], 475).

⁴Richard C. Steiner, "Does the Biblical Hebrew Conjunction ו- Have Many Meanings, One Meaning, or No Meaning At All?," *JBL* 119 (2000): 249–67 at 256.

⁵Steiner, "Biblical Hebrew Conjunction," 260.

⁶Steiner points to the careful nuance used in BDB to state, "It connects *contrasted* ideas, where in our idiom the contrast would be expressed explicitly by *but*, in such cases prominence is usually given to the contrasted idea by it being placed immediately after the conjunction" ("Biblical Hebrew Conjunction," 260).

5.2.1 Two Hebrew Break Structures

Due to the necessity of examining context, this study is limited to two structures involving *vav* which Hebrew commonly uses to signal a contrast. Randall Buth introduces the first structure, "וְדָבָר פָּעַל marks a break in a story by not using the sequential tenses."[7] Garrett and DeRouchie go on to note that Hebrew commonly uses the break structure "*vav* + X + verb" for contrastive matching.[8] Though this structure can mark contrasting items, it serves multiple other functions in Hebrew prose. Fuller describes how this structure, actually a form of nominal clause, turns the attention towards "description" and less towards action.[9] Genesis 37:11 provides an example of this structure:

"And his brothers hated him,	וַיְקַנְאוּ־בוֹ אֶחָיו
but his father kept the matter."	וְאָבִיו שָׁמַר אֶת־הַדָּבָר׃

The *vav* + X + verb sequence in the second half of the verse stops the forward momentum of the narrative to offer an item of contrast. Buth writes, "For Hebrew and Aramaic syntactic studies it will prove easier in the long run to use terms like continuity and discontinuity as a

---

[7] Randall Buth, *Living Biblical Hebrew ג: Selected Readings with 500 Friends* (Jerusalem: Biblical Language Center, 2006), 161. Buth understands Hebrew to be a VSO language that places marked constituents before the verb. See also Randall Buth, "Functional Grammar, Hebrew and Aramaic: An Integrated Textlinguistic Approach to Syntax," in *Discourse Analysis of Biblical Literature: What it is, and What it Offers*, ed. Walter J. Bodine (Atlanta: Scholars Press, 1995), 77–102 at 80.

[8] This is only one of multiple functions listed for an "offline" clause. Contrastive matching specifically occurs when a verb initial clause precedes this formation: Verb + X // X + Verb (Duane A. Garrett and Jason S. DeRouchie, *A Modern Grammar for Biblical Hebrew* [Nashville: B&H, 2009], 296, 288).

[9] Russell T. Fuller and Kyoungwon Choi, *Invitation to Biblical Hebrew Syntax: An Intermediate Grammar* (Grand Rapids: Kregel, 2016), Syntax §38.V.

replacement for the pragmatically defined foreground and background. The *waw ha-hippuk* is the tense-aspect system to mark continuity, while the [X + verb] structures are the system to mark discontinuity."[10] This nominal structure, beginning with a *vav*, alerts readers to be aware of discontinuity in the narrative—and often this discontinuity expresses some sort of contrast.[11]

A second common break structure, generally used to indicate a simple negative statement, also indicates contrast. The *vav* + לא + verb sequence introduces a discontinuity in the flow of narrative in order to highlight a contrast between two statements.[12] The context will once again prove the decisive factor in alerting readers to a potential contrast, with *vav* standing at the point of polarity. Genesis 31:7 provides an example of *vav* immediately preceding the adverb לא for contrast:

| "And your father deceived me and changed my wages ten times, but God did not permit him to do evil to me." | וַאֲבִיכֶן הֵתֶל בִּי וְהֶחֱלִף אֶת־מַשְׂכֻּרְתִּי עֲשֶׂרֶת מֹנִים וְלֹא־נְתָנוֹ אֱלֹהִים לְהָרַע עִמָּדִי׃ |

---

[10] Buth, "Functional Grammar," 99.

[11] Bill T. Arnold and John H. Choi, *A Guide to Biblical Hebrew Syntax* (New York: Cambridge University Press, 2003), 146; Aaron Hornkohl, "The Pragmatics of the X-Verb Structure in the Hebrew of Genesis: The Linguistic Functions and Associated Effects and Meanings of Intra-Clausal Fronted Constituents" (M.A. thesis, Hebrew University, 2003), 38–39; Fuller and Choi, *Biblical Hebrew Syntax*, Syntax §38.

[12] Fuller and Choi, *Biblical Hebrew Syntax*, Syntax §6.A.1.b. Compare to Moshavi's categories of "focus of negation" and "focus with negation." These categories deal with לא before a preposed noun phrase (focus of negation) or לא before a verb after a preposed noun phrase (focus with negation) (Adina M. Moshavi, *Word Order in the Biblical Hebrew Finite Clause: A Syntactic and Pragmatic Analysis of Preposing* [Winona Lake, IN: Eisenbrauns, 2010], §8.4).

CHAPTER 5: ACCENTS AT CONTRAST STRUCTURES   117

If this passage indicated a simple negative statement in line three, Jacob might have said something to the effect of, "(positive) he changed my wages ten times, (negative) and did not give me my annual bonus." In this way the speaker describes both a positive and a negative action, each standing on its own, "he did X, and he did not do Y." But when this structure indicates a contrast, the second statement must run in opposition to the first statement, or at least the reader's expectation of what should follow the first statement—"he did X, but then (contrary to our expectations) he did not do Y." Thus, this structure that often breaks the narrative as a simple negative many also indicate a contrast.

5.2.2   CONTRAST VIA BREAK STRUCTURES

These passages from Genesis illustrate two ways that context signals the presence of a contrast: the break structure *vav* + X + verb, and the *vav* + לא + verb sequence. These structures also serve other functions in Hebrew. The first break structure, *vav* + X + verb, serves generally as a focus marker. Buth divides the function of this structure into contextualization (topic) and focus.[13] Hornkohl builds on this by offering more specific functions within these two categories, contrast being a focal function.[14] Fuller, in more traditional terms, describes this structure as a nominal clause that describes, emphasizes, contrasts, and clarifies the initiator (X) of the clause.[15] The book of Judges provides numerous examples of how this structure indicates a change of

---

[13] Buth, "Functional Grammar," 84.
[14] Hornkohl, "Pragmatics of the X-Verb Structure," 38. Cf. Moshavi, *Word Order in the Biblical Hebrew Finite Clause*, §3.3.1.3.
[15] Fuller and Choi, *Biblical Hebrew Syntax*, Syntax §38.IV. See also Joshua Jacobson, *Chanting the Hebrew Bible: The Art of Cantillation* (Philadelphia: Jewish Publication Society, 2002), 483–84.

characters (3:26), offers the result of previous action (4:3), and provides background information in the form of parallelism (13:2). Thus, while the form may be objectively signaled, the reader must still make contextual decisions regarding function.

The second break structure, *vav* + לא + verb, likewise serves multiple functions. This structure indicates a range of negations, from a simple negative clause, to prohibitions, absolute and categorical negations.[16] The book of Judges contains numerous positive-negative statements (2:20; 3:28–29; 6:5; 11:35; 14:16). Yet, these negative clauses do not necessarily indicate contrast. A contrast requires the direct intersection of two statements based upon a shared factor. For example, "I like apples; and I do not play baseball." These positive and negative assertions stand side by side, but they do not contrast with one another because there is no shared feature. But, to say, "I like apples; but I do not eat oranges," does offer a contrast. Here the category of "fruit" draws these two statements into contrast with one another. This comprises the subjective element in this study, discerning when either of these break structures indicates contrast.

5.3   *SUMMARY OF DATA*

While Hebrew uses numerous contrast particles and patterns, including just a bare *vav* between clauses, this study will focus on the use of two contrast sequences in the book of Judges: the break structure *vav* + X + verb, and the *vav* + לא + verb sequence.[17] This dissertation seeks

---

[16]Fuller and Choi, *Biblical Hebrew Syntax*, Syntax §42.

[17]I do not categorically reject the nomenclature "adversative *vav*," but determining such uses of *vav* often produces varied results. Translations differ widely, and the LXX generally prefers the use of καὶ for *vav*, even in clearly contrastive contexts. While the contrast structures presented here include *vav* and are open to the

foremost to examine how the accents work in contexts of contrast, not to study Hebrew contrast structures—hence the limitation of this study to these two structures. These contrast structures provide an objective starting point for determining contrast relationships between clauses. While not every occurrence of these structures necessarily indicates a contrast, they provide a syntactic signal that requires the reader to evaluate the relationship of clauses more carefully. Observing how the Masoretes accent these contrast structures may prove a fertile starting place for future examinations of how the Masoretes treat other forms of contrast.[18]

Table 42 presents the occurrences of these two break structures used to mark a contrast throughout the book of Judges. Structure #1 (*vav* + X + verb) signals a contrast relationship 26 percent of time in a verse initial position, 39 percent of the time after Etnachta, and 35 percent of the time after Zaqef. Structure #2 (*vav* + לא + verb) signals a contrast relationship 26 percent of the time in a verse initial position, 48 percent of the time after Etnachta, 15 percent of the time after Zaqef, and 11 percent of the time with other accents. For both structures, Etnachta stands at the point of contrast more than any other accent. Nevertheless, this falls far short of a 75 percent threshold for indicating an intentional pattern on the part of the Masoretes.[19]

---

same criticism of subjectivity, the range of options narrows significantly.

[18] This dissertation describes Masoretic work actively (see ch. 1, n. 7).

[19] Even if the verse initial examples are removed from the study, the percentages are still much lower than 75 percent. This chapter will consider whether this meets the standard of intentional pattern under "Outline of the Masoretic Approach."

Table 42. Accents occurring at contrast structures

Verse Initial	Etnachta	Zaqef	Other
Structure #1: *vav* + X + verb			
1:21; 2:17; 3:19; 10:13; 20:40; 21:18	1:8; 1:25; 1:28; 7:6; 7:25; 18:27; 19:16; 19:24; 20:34	6:39; 6:40; 7:4; 7:8; 11:27; 15:13; 16:20; 20:42	
Structure #2: *vav* + לֹא / אֵין			
1:27; 9:20; 11:20; 11:28; 14:13; 19:10; 19:25	2:2; 4:8; 6:10; 8:20; 9:15; 11:18; 13:6; 14:6; 14:9; 14:14; 15:1; 20:13; 21:14	12:2; 13:9; 19:15; 19:18	11:17—Revia 11:17—Tipecha 19:28—Tipecha

For the sake of comparison, table 43 presents two common adversative conjunctions (כִּי אִם, אוּלָם). Because Hebrew narrative tends to use these conjunctions sparingly, this table includes a sample from Genesis through Kings. The contrast marker כי אם occurs at similar rates when compared with the contrast structure data from the book of Judges. The contrast marker אולם, however, exhibits a much stronger influence on the accents, only occurring in the verse initial position or after Etnachta. Other than כי אם, each contrast form pairs most commonly with Etnachta.

Table 43. Location of other common adversatives

Verse Initial	Etnachta	Zaqef	Other
כִּי אִם			
Exod 23:22; Num 24:22; Deut 7:5; 12:5; 12:14; 12:18; 16:6; Josh 23:8; 1 Kgs 20:6; 2 Kgs 17:36; 17:39; 23:23	Gen 15:4; Exod 12:9; Lev 21:14; Num 10:30; 1 Sam 21:4; 2 Sam 13:33; 1 Kgs 8:19; 22:3; 2 Kgs 17:40; 23:9	Gen 32:28; 1 Sam 8:19; 2 Sam 5:6; 1 Kgs 18:18; 2 Kgs 14:6	Gen 35:10; Num 26:33; Josh 17:3; 2 Sam 21:2
אוּלָם			
Exod 9:16; Num 14:21; 1 Sam 25:34	Gen 28:19; 48:19; Judg 18:29; 1 Sam 20:3; 1 Kgs 20:23		

Nevertheless, no singular pattern emerges as predominant. Thus, one may initially conclude from this data that no intentional pattern exists for how the Masoretes chose to accent contrast clauses, whether indicated by contrast structures or conjunctions (see also table 44 for a statistical comparison of these four structures).

Table 44. Comparison of contrast structure and accent occurrence rates

	Verse Initial (%)	Etnachta (%)	Zaqef (%)	Other (%)
Structure #1	26	39	35	--
Structure #2	26	48	15	11
כִּי אִם	39	32	16	13
אוּלָם	37	63	--	--

However, analyzing this same data from another perspective sheds some more light on what the Masoretes actually do with contrast clauses. Table 45 provides a breakdown of possible factors that influence the accentuation of contrast clauses. First, notice that other Masoretic accent patterns (i.e., the conclusion of direct speech and conditional clauses) determined the flow of the accentuation in 18 of 50 examples. So, a full 36 percent of contrast clauses occur in passages where they are dominated by another accent pattern. Due to the syntactic significance of these other patterns, the weakness of a contrast relationship cannot compete for the major disjunctive slot. Second, when Etnachta groups clauses instead highlight a contrast, Zaqef or other lower level accents stand before a contrast clause. In other words, Etnachta groups the contrast clause proper in the same half-verse with its object of contrast; all other verse components reside in the other half-verse.

CHAPTER 5: ACCENTS AT CONTRAST STRUCTURES

Table 45. Determining factors for accenting contrast clauses

	Direct Speech	Clausal Groupings	Semantic Weight
Structure #1			
Verse Initial	20:40	--	1:21; 2:17; 3:19; 10:13; 21:18
Etnachta	--	1:28; 7:6; 20:34	1:8; 1:25; 7:25; 18:27; 19:16; 19:24
Zaqef	15:13; 16:20	6:39; 6:40; 7:4; 7:8; 11:27; 20:42	--
Structure #2			
Verse Initial	9:20*; 11:20; 11:28; 14:13*; 19:10; 19:25	--	1:27
Etnachta	2:2; 4:8*; 6:10; 8:20; 9:15*; 14:14; 15:1; 20:13	13:6; 14:6	11:18; 14:9; 21:14
Zaqef/Other	19:28	11:17 (x2); 12:2; 13:9; 19:15; 19:18	--

*Indicates a conditional clause, otherwise all examples relate to direct speech.

Third, on numerous occasions the Masoretes position the major disjunctive immediately before a contrast clause which comprises the main point in the verse. That is to say, the contrast forms the most important aspect of what the verse communicates. In general, each of these semantic placements could situate the major disjunction elsewhere in the verse, but the sense points to the priority of the contrast.

This data seems to indicate that though a singular pattern cannot define how the Masoretes accented contrast clauses, the Masoretes tend to give contrast structures a prominent position in their consideration for accentuation. In other words, an intentional pattern may not exist, but the Masoretes certainly pay attention to contrast structures. This proposal differs significantly from the other three in this dissertation. Therefore, this proposal first requires evidence that the Masoretes give significant attention to a contrast clause. Second, this proposal grows clearer in light of examples demonstrating the various reasons the Masoretes did not give attention to a contrast clause in the verse.

5.4 OUTLINE OF THE MASORETIC APPROACH

The Masoretes take notice of contrast structures in their positioning of the accents. The clearest evidence of their awareness comes from examples where the contrast structure stands at a semantic point of interest. Notice from table 45 that throughout the book of Judges, the Masoretes never use Zaqef or lower accents on contrast structures that bear the semantic weight of a passage. In other words, when the Masoretes understand the contrast structure to comprise the most salient portion of the verse, they pair it with a strong accent (unless another pattern makes this impossible). The low percentage rate for these examples arises not from Masoretic inconsistency on this matter, but from the relatively few number of verses where a contrast structure alone forms the most important semantic point of a verse.[20]

---

[20] All biblical examples will appear in tables and the discussion will generally refer to them by their biblical reference location, not by table number.

5.4.1 CONTRAST STRUCTURE #1: VAV + X + VERB

Items of great semantic significance occur at the beginning of the verse, as well as with Etnachta in the middle of the verse. Judges 2:17 provides an example of the narrator using a contrast structure at the beginning of a verse. This example only makes sense in relation to the context.

Table 46. Structure #1 example: Judges 2:17

Action	וַיָּ֧קֶם יְהוָ֛ה שֹֽׁפְטִ֖ים	16a
Action	וַיּ֣וֹשִׁיע֔וּם מִיַּ֖ד שֹׁסֵיהֶֽם׃	16b
Contrast Structure	וְגַ֥ם אֶל־שֹׁפְטֵיהֶ֖ם לֹ֣א שָׁמֵ֑עוּ	17a
Grounding Clause	כִּ֣י זָנ֗וּ אַֽחֲרֵי֙ אֱלֹהִ֣ים אֲחֵרִ֔ים	17b
(cont.)	וַיִּֽשְׁתַּחֲו֖וּ לָהֶ֑ם	17c
Explanation	סָ֣רוּ מַהֵ֗ר מִן־הַדֶּ֜רֶךְ אֲשֶׁ֨ר הָלְכ֧וּ אֲבוֹתָ֛ם	17d
	לִשְׁמֹ֥עַ מִצְוֺת־יְהוָ֖ה	--
Comparison Clause	לֹא־עָ֥שׂוּ כֵֽן׃	17e

The narrator clearly intends 17a to make a strong statement: "And YHWH raised up judges (16a), and they delivered [Israel] from the hand of their plunderers (16b). But even to their judges [Israel] did not listen (17a)." The initial clause in 17a contrasts sharply with v.16 (e.g., emphatic use of גַם). An entire verse follows this clause in order to rationalize the contrast. Not only does the narrator ground his initial claim (17b, c), he offers further explanation to drive home the point (17d, e). Such development to support the contrast indicates that the contrastive nature of 17a was a major point within the overall discourse.

Such semantic contrasts not only occur in the extended voice of the narrator, but also within the direct speech of characters. In Judges 10:13, God speaks to the people of Israel in a speech that extends across four verses.

Table 47. Structure #1 example: Judges 10:13

Intro to DS	וַיֹּ֤אמֶר יְהוָה֙ אֶל־בְּנֵ֣י יִשְׂרָאֵ֔ל	11a
Rhetorical Q	הֲלֹ֤א מִמִּצְרַ֙יִם֙ וּמִן־הָ֣אֱמֹרִ֔י	11b
	וּמִן־בְּנֵ֥י עַמּ֖וֹן וּמִן־פְּלִשְׁתִּֽים׃	--
Question (cont.)	וְצִידוֹנִ֤ים וַֽעֲמָלֵק֙ וּמָע֔וֹן לָחֲצ֖וּ אֶתְכֶ֑ם	12-
	וַתִּצְעֲק֣וּ אֵלַ֔י	12a
Result	וָאוֹשִׁ֥יעָה אֶתְכֶ֖ם מִיָּדָֽם׃	12b
Contrast	וְאַתֶּם֙ עֲזַבְתֶּ֣ם אוֹתִ֔י	13a
	וַתַּעַבְד֖וּ אֱלֹהִ֣ים אֲחֵרִ֑ים	13b
Conclusion	לָכֵ֥ן לֹא־אוֹסִ֖יף לְהוֹשִׁ֥יעַ אֶתְכֶֽם׃	13c

The verse contains two components: (1) the contrast indictment (13a, b), and (2) the conclusion to the rhetorical question (13c). The contrast structure operates within the overall rhetorical question (11b–13b) and sets the stage for the ultimate conclusion (13c). In other words, the contrast may not be the main point of the entire speech (that comes in 13c), but the contrast of 13a is the main hinge of the extended rhetorical question. Thus, the Masoretes appropriately make sure that this rhetorical hinge occurs at a verse juncture. Verse initial positioning may prove significant semantically.

Such verse initial points of interest require looking beyond the verse for the item of contrast. But often the entire contrast package appears within a single verse. Judges 7:25 illustrates this type of contrast structure.

Table 48. Structure #1 example: Judges 7:25

Initial Action	וַֽיִּלְכְּד֞וּ שְׁנֵֽי־שָׂרֵ֤י מִדְיָן֙ אֶת־עֹרֵ֣ב וְאֶת־זְאֵ֔ב	25a
Parallel Line A	וַיַּהַרְג֤וּ אֶת־עוֹרֵב֙ בְּצוּר־עוֹרֵ֔ב	25b
Parallel Line B	וְאֶת־זְאֵ֛ב הָרְג֥וּ בְיֶֽקֶב־זְאֵ֖ב	25c
Resultant Action	וַֽיִּרְדְּפ֖וּ אֶל־מִדְיָ֑ן	25d
Contrast Structure	וְרֹאשׁ־עֹרֵ֣ב וּזְאֵ֗ב הֵבִ֙יאוּ֙ אֶל־גִּדְע֔וֹן מֵעֵ֖בֶר לַיַּרְדֵּֽן׃	25e

Interestingly, this verse provides two examples of the *vav* + X + verb structure (25c, e). The first example may superficially appear to be a contrast, "And they killed Orev at the Rock of Orev, (vav) Ze'ev they killed at the Winepress of Ze'ev" (25c). But the X + verb structure can do far more than indicate contrast. In this case, 25c better illustrates the use of this structure to bring two events into parallel without respect to sequence. Hornkohl writes, "The fronting of an element often involves marking of more than just the fronted element itself. [At times] ... comparison or contrast of the fronted constituents is not the point. Rather, the entire clause is marked in order to generally parallelize referents and events."[21] In this case, the author puts the death of Orev and Ze'ev in parallel, though they likely did not occur at the same time.

---

[21]Hornkohl, "The Pragmatics of the X-Verb Structure," 45.

The more important example of the *vav* + X + verb occurs in 25e where a clear contrast is drawn with the previous action in 25d. Here the actions are contrasted using two different verbs and two different structures. As far as the accentuation, since every clause in this verse describes actions by the same 3MP group of men, the Masoretes have a lot of freedom as to where they could place Etnachta. A logical position appears after 25c. This would group the two statements being contrasted in 25d and 25e in the second half-verse; it would also separate the act of killing these two Midianite princes from subsequent actions. Instead, the Masoretes place Etnachta right at the point of contrast, "they pursued after Midian, [Etnachta] but the head of Orev and Ze'ev they brought to Gideon across the Jordan." After this point the entire narrative takes a strange turn. The battle recedes into the background, and a quarrel arises between Gideon and the men of Ephraim. So, the effort by the Masoretes to highlight this contrast with Etnachta signals more than just a turn in the verse or the events of the battle, it draws attention to a major transition in the Gideon narrative.

5.4.2   CONTRAST STRUCTURE #2: *VAV* + לא + VERB

The second contrast structure, *vav* + לא + verb, commonly sits at the head of a verse. But very few of these examples illustrate a point of semantic interest. Judges 1:27 shows how this contrast structure can highlight a point of great semantic relevance at the beginning of a verse. The first chapter of Judges is divided into various smaller units using Setumah and Petuchah. The verse initial contrast structure follows a Petuchah break at the end of v.26. The previous section (vv.22–26) recounts the success of the tribes of Joseph in capturing the city of Bethel—"but Menasheh did not dispossess ..." (27a). The list in v.27

acts as a powerful condemnation for their failure to press their success to its appointed conclusion—"and the Canaanites were determined to dwell in this land" (27b). This failure has already arisen in 1:19 and 1:21, but here the narrator digs in deeper. The list following the initial statement of failure shows the dramatic nature of this debacle. Hence, the Petuchah break coupled with this verse initial contrast structure indicates that the narrator intends to portray the weight of this failure.

Table 49. Structure #2 example: Judges 1:27

Contrast Structure	וְלֹא־הוֹרִישׁ מְנַשֶּׁה אֶת־בֵּית־שְׁאָן וְאֶת־בְּנוֹתֶיהָ	27a
List of Nations	וְאֶת־תַּעְנַךְ וְאֶת־בְּנֹתֶיהָ	--
	וְאֶת־יֹשֵׁב דוֹר וְאֶת־בְּנוֹתֶיהָ	--
	וְאֶת־יוֹשְׁבֵי יִבְלְעָם וְאֶת־בְּנֹתֶיהָ	--
Delayed Etnachta (list)	וְאֶת־יוֹשְׁבֵי מְגִדּוֹ וְאֶת־בְּנוֹתֶיהָ	--
Result	וַיּוֹאֶל הַכְּנַעֲנִי לָשֶׁבֶת בָּאָרֶץ הַזֹּאת׃	27b

As with the first contrast structure, the Masoretes will pair Etnachta with the point of contrast whenever this comprises the most salient aspect of the verse. In Judges 11:15–27, Jephthah writes a letter to the king of the Ammonites. At multiple points Jephthah uses the *vav* + לֹא + verb break structure to indicate a contrast. While 11:17 and 11:20 record contrasting reactions, Jephthah makes one of his more important arguments in 11:18. The Ammonite king accuses Israel of taking territory from Ammon when they came out Egypt (11:13). Jephthah refutes this claim with his long narrative showing that Israel never even entered the land of Moab, Ammon's neighbor.

With its multiple sequential clauses, this verse provides an excellent example of Masoretic choice in positioning the accents. The Masoretes could have sensibly placed Etnachta after 18c, broken the verse evenly, and put the two clauses being contrasted in the second half-verse (18d, e). As it stands, the Masoretes grouped the contrast clause (18e) and the grounding clause (18f) distinctly from the previous chain of actions. This places Etnachta on the point of contrast and draws more attention to the break structure. Jephthah employs these contrast structures in order to refute the Ammonite basis for invading Israel. The Masoretes use the accents to highlight Jephthah's rhetorical effort.

Table 50. Structure #2 example: Judges 11:18

Action	וַיֵּ֣לֶךְ בַּמִּדְבָּ֗ר	18a
Action	וַיָּ֜סָב אֶת־אֶ֤רֶץ אֱדוֹם֙ וְאֶת־אֶ֣רֶץ מוֹאָ֔ב	18b
Action	וַיָּבֹ֤א מִמִּזְרַח־שֶׁ֙מֶשׁ֙ לְאֶ֣רֶץ מוֹאָ֔ב	18c
Action	וַֽיַּחֲנ֖וּן בְּעֵ֣בֶר אַרְנ֑וֹן	18d
Contrast Structure	וְלֹא־בָ֙אוּ֙ בִּגְב֣וּל מוֹאָ֔ב	18e
Grounding Clause	כִּ֥י אַרְנ֖וֹן גְּב֥וּל מוֹאָֽב׃	18f

A very similar example occurs in Judges 14:9 where a string of actions culminates in a contrast structure. Samson was born under a Nazarite vow which involved growing his hair long, avoiding all produce of the grapevine, and not touching a dead body (Num 6:1–8). But Samson regularly breaks these commands. As with most stories in the Bible, the narrator rarely states a direct condemnation of the characters. Instead, the narrator expects the reader to notice the wrongdoing of a character according to background knowledge of the Mosaic law (cf. Deut 17:14–20 and 1 Kgs 10:26–11:3).

Table 51. Structure #2 example: Judges 14:9

Action	וַיִּרְדֵּהוּ אֶל־כַּפָּיו	9a
Action	וַיֵּלֶךְ הָלוֹךְ וְאָכֹל	9b
Action	וַיֵּלֶךְ אֶל־אָבִיו וְאֶל־אִמּוֹ	9c
Action	וַיִּתֵּן לָהֶם	9d
Action	וַיֹּאכֵלוּ	9e
Contrast Structure	וְלֹא־הִגִּיד לָהֶם	9f
Content Clause	כִּי מִגְּוִיַּת הָאַרְיֵה רָדָה הַדְּבָשׁ:	9g

Here the narrator records a string of Samson's actions and then introduces a break structure in 9f in order to offer a comment. He could have continued the string of *vayiqtol* clauses and just made 9f another action in the story. But by using the break structure he draws attention to this important fact—Samson kept his unlawful actions a secret, knowing that he was in violation of his vows. The Masoretes likely saw this effort by the narrator and choose to pair Etnachta with the contrast structure in order to further alert the reader to the significance of this comment.

The Masoretes also choose semantic points of contrast in more limited contexts as well. In Judges 21:14, the Masoretes can only choose between two positions in the verse for the position of Etnachta. The first clause records the action of the remnant of Benjamin; the second clause records the action of Israel. The contrast structure follows these two initial clauses with a rather undefined 3MP subject. Most likely this subject remains the Israelites of 14b, "but they had not found a corresponding amount for them."[22] However one chooses to translate 14c, this clause closely contrasts with 14b; the action of giving reveals the failure of finding. The Masoretes split these clauses with Etnachta rather than grouping them together (cf. Judg 20:42 later in the chapter). In effect the Masoretes tie the first two clauses together and position Etnachta to draw attention to the contrast. Further, this contrast point sets up the final controversy-laden episode in Judges 21:16–24.

Table 52. Structure #2 example: Judges 21:14

Action (group #1)	וַיָּ֣שָׁב בִּנְיָמִ֔ן בָּעֵ֖ת הַהִ֑יא	14a
Action (group #2)	וַיִּתְּנ֤וּ לָהֶם֙ הַנָּשִׁ֔ים אֲשֶׁ֣ר חִיּ֔וּ מִנְּשֵׁ֖י יָבֵ֣שׁ גִּלְעָ֑ד	14b
Contrast Structure	וְלֹֽא־מָצְא֥וּ לָהֶ֖ם כֵּֽן׃	14c

These examples from the book of Judges illustrate how the Masoretes place semantically significant contrasts at the beginning of the verse or pair them with Etnachta. Each contrast proved to be significant in the overall narrative. Many of the examples provided the Masoretes with multiple, legitimate accentuation schemes, thereby further indicating their intentional choice in positioning Etnachta. Thus, when a semantically significant contrast occurs in a verse without competing syntactical formations, the Masoretes highlight the contrast.

---

[22]Hebrew perfects commonly render into English as past perfect verbs, especially in narrative contexts (Fuller and Choi, *Biblical Hebrew Syntax*, Syntax §3.B.3.a.iii). See also Daniel I. Block, *Judges, Ruth,* NAC 6 (Nashville: B&H, 1999), 577.

5.5 *DIVERGENCE FROM THE APPROACH*

Despite the Masoretic tendency to highlight contrast structures where possible, more often than not these syntactic formations find themselves outranked. Other patterns of deploying the accents (e.g., concluding mid-verse direct speech, framing conditional clauses) exert more influence over the meaning of the verse. Thus, when contrasts occur in the same verse as these formations, the contrast structure will receive a lower level accent. Similarly, the grouping of clauses often proves more significant to the correct reading of a verse than highlighting a contrast structure. In these situations, pairing Etnachta with the contrast structure would introduce more confusion than clarity. Further, many examples of contrast structures only influence the interpretation on a small scale, they do not guide the direction of the overall passage (cf. Judg 7:25; 11:18). Because these displacement factors occur more often than semantically significant contrasts, it does not seem prudent to label the accentuation of contrasts as an intentional Masoretic pattern. Nevertheless, contrast remains an influential consideration for accentuation.

5.5.1 PRIORITY OF ANOTHER PATTERN

Certain Masoretic patterns of accentuation bear more weight than others. The Masoretes prioritize accenting the conclusion of mid-verse direct speech and the framing of conditional clauses over contrast clauses. Whenever these features occur in the same verse, these patterns will receive the principle accents. Judges 16:20 illustrates how accenting mid-verse direct speech often dominates the list of priorities.

Table 53. Alternate pattern example: Judges 16:20

Intro to DS	וַתֹּאמֶר	20a
DS (emphatic warning)	פְּלִשְׁתִּים עָלֶיךָ שִׁמְשׁוֹן	20b
Action (change of character)	וַיִּקַץ מִשְּׁנָתוֹ	20c
Intro to Self-speech	וַיֹּאמֶר	20d
DS (self-speech)	אֵצֵא כְּפַעַם בְּפַעַם	20e
DS (self-speech)	וְאִנָּעֵר	20f
Contrast Structure #1	וְהוּא לֹא יָדַע	20g
Content Clause	כִּי יְהוָה סָר מֵעָלָיו׃	20h

This verse represents the fourth and final test Delilah puts to Samson. As she has done before, she issues a warning about the Philistines ready to attack Samson (cf. 16:9, 12, 14). This line of direct speech, though very early in the verse, draws the strongest accent (20b). After that point the narrative switches to Samson's actions, another possible reason that strongest accent appears in 20b. But 20f contains the conclusion of mid-verse "direct speech," as well as introducing a contrast comment from the narrator.[23] While this juncture forms the strongest break in the second half of the verse, the Masoretes give more importance to the emphatic exclamation of Delilah.

---

[23]The choice by the Masoretes may also be influenced by the possibility that Samson's "speech" is actually his thoughts, or self-speech. The first person verbs and the niphal form of the second verb indicate that it is likely Samson merely thought these ideas to himself and did not audibly say the words (Trent C. Butler, *Judges*, WBC 8 [Nashville: Thomas Nelson, 2009], 310; Block, *Judges, Ruth*, 461).

The pattern of pairing Etnachta with the conclusion of mid-verse direct speech also takes precedent over contrast clauses that occur within the direct speech. In Judges 15:13, the men of Judah are about to turn Samson over to the Philistines. Samson grows concerned that his kinsmen will assassinate him on behalf of the Philistines, in which case he would probably fight them. But these men reassure him, "we will bind you, and give you into their hands, but we *certainly* will not kill you." The infinitive absolute, a verbal noun, stands before the negative particle (13e). The infinitive absolute functions here as an absolute object to emphasize the certainty of the verb.[24]

Table 54. Alternate pattern example: Judges 15:13

Intro to DS	וַיֹּאמְרוּ לוֹ לֵאמֹר	13a
Negative Answer to Question	לֹא ↘	13b
Positive Answer; Contrast (כִּי)	כִּי־אָסֹר נֶאֱסָרְךָ	13c
Answer	וּנְתַנּוּךָ בְיָדָם	13d
Contrast Structure	וְהָמֵת לֹא נְמִיתֶךָ	13e
Follow-up Action	וַיַּאַסְרֻהוּ בִּשְׁנַיִם עֲבֹתִים חֲדָשִׁים	13f
Follow-up Action	וַיַּעֲלוּהוּ מִן־הַסָּלַע׃	13g

Thus, these men offer Samson an emphatic promise, "we will do X and Y, but certainly not Z." In light of this strong statement, the Masoretes could conceivably place Etnachta before this contrast structure (13d). But overall, the verse demands that Etnachta mark the end of direct

---

[24]Fuller and Choi, *Biblical Hebrew Syntax*, Syntax §13.A.1.

speech. Instead, the Masoretes pair Zaqef, the strongest accent of the half-verse, with the contrast clause.

Quite often the point of contrast occurs at the same location in the verse as the conclusion of direct speech. Either the narrator will offer a contrastive statement to what was just spoken in direct speech, or the speaker will react contrastively to something in the speech they quoted. Judges 2:2 records an example of God chastising the people for their faithlessness.[25] The quoted words in this passage conclude mid-verse (2b) before the comments of the speaker resume (2c). The commentary resumes with a contrast structure. For, contrary to the hopes and expectations of the reader, Israel has discarded the promise and disobeyed the commands. The collision of these two syntactic features makes it difficult to determine which exerts more influence.

Table 55. Alternate pattern example: Judges 2:2

Intro to Quoted DS	וַאֹמַ֖ר	1e
DS Promise	לֹא־אָפֵ֧ר בְּרִיתִ֛י אִתְּכֶ֖ם לְעוֹלָֽם׃	1f
DS Command	וְאַתֶּ֗ם לֹא־תִכְרְת֤וּ בְרִית֙ לְיֽוֹשְׁבֵי֙ הָאָ֣רֶץ הַזֹּ֔את	2a
DS Command	מִזְבְּחוֹתֵיהֶ֖ם תִּתֹּצ֑וּן	2b
Contrast Structure	וְלֹֽא־שְׁמַעְתֶּ֥ם בְּקֹלִ֖י	2c
Exclamation	מַה־זֹּ֥את עֲשִׂיתֶֽם׃	2d

---

[25]See ch. 2 of this dissertation for a discussion of Judg 15:1 and 19:28, excellent examples of direct speech ending with a contrastive comment by the narrator. An illustration of direct speech ending at Sof Pasuq occurs at Judg 11:28 and the next verse begins with a contrast structure. See also Judg 20:39–40 for an example of a contrast beginning a verse after the conclusion of direct speech in the previous verse.

From elsewhere, evidence shows that signaling the conclusion of mid-verse direct speech constitutes an intentional pattern. But were this verse to be restated in the Hebrew without quoted speech, the position of Etnachta would likely remain the same. The contrast stands at the most significant milestone in this passage of direct speech (2:1–3). In other words, the Hebrew Bible contains numerous examples of pragmatic accentuation according to prevailing patterns that also constitute semantic points of interest when examined in light of a different syntactic feature.

This dictum rings true for direct speech and conditional statements alike. A number of passages that clearly operate according to the pattern of framing conditional statements also include an example of a contrast structure. Judges 4:8 records Baraq's response to Deborah's prophesy.[26] According to the pattern of framing conditional statements, the accent concluding the apodosis will be the direct superior to the concluding accent of the protasis.

Table 56. Alternate pattern example: Judges 4:8

Intro to DS	וַיֹּ֤אמֶר אֵלֶ֙יהָ֙ בָּרָ֔ק	8a
Protasis #1	אִם־תֵּלְכִ֥י עִמִּ֖י ↘	8b
Apodosis #1	וְהָלָ֑כְתִּי	8c
Protasis #2 (contrast structure)	וְאִם־לֹ֥א תֵלְכִ֖י עִמִּ֖י ↘	8d
Apodosis #2	לֹ֥א אֵלֵֽךְ׃	8e

---

[26]See Judg 9:19–20 for a verse initial example much like this passage.

In this case the first protasis concludes with Tipecha, subordinate to Etnachta. Conveniently this juncture also leads into a contrast statement. While the statistically stronger pattern of conditional frames likely dictated the location of Etnachta, the tendency to highlight points of contrast adds another hammer blow. Thus, knowledge of what the Masoretes tend to highlight, even if statistically weak, elucidates their choice of accentuation and their understanding of the passage.

5.5.2 THE DIVISION OF CLAUSES

The Masoretes prioritize certain patterns over others, and certain syntactic features over others (Judg 15:13; 16:20). At times these patterns nicely co-operate with one another making their influence indistinguishable (Judg 2:2; 4:8). This dynamic also operates on verses where clause-grouping exerts significant weight on the meaning of the passage. The Masoretes often deploy the accents to properly group clauses so as to clarify the meaning of the text. While this rarely brings about divergence from stronger patterns, quite regularly this consideration displaces the Masoretic tendency to pair contrast statements with Etnachta.[27]

Judges 11:17 illustrates the Masoretic choice of clausal groupings over the contrast structure they contain. This verse records two main actions (שלח, ישב), each actions receiving a half-verse unit. The first half-verse unit contains two parallel actions, both using the same verb (17a, d). The break structure in 17d does not indicate contrast but functions to put these two activities in parallel (cf. Judg 7:25). The break structures in 17c and 17e indicate contrast with the previous line.

---

[27] Note the examples of clause division based divergence provided in ch. 3 and 4 of this dissertation.

Table 57. Division of clauses example: Judges 11:17

Action #1a	וַיִּשְׁלַח יִשְׂרָאֵל מַלְאָכִים ׀ אֶל־מֶלֶךְ אֱדוֹם ׀ לֵאמֹר	17a
DS Request	אֶעְבְּרָה־נָּא בְאַרְצֶךָ	17b
Response #1a	וְלֹא שָׁמַע מֶלֶךְ אֱדוֹם	17c
Action #1b	וְגַם אֶל־מֶלֶךְ מוֹאָב שָׁלַח	17d
Response #1b	וְלֹא אָבָה	17e
Action #2	וַיֵּשֶׁב יִשְׂרָאֵל בְּקָדֵשׁ:	17f

Thus, the Masoretes group two parallel requests ("let us pass through your land"), and two parallel rejections ("no!"). In their understanding, grouping these together as one unit contributes more to the clarity and meaning of the verse than would highlighting the contrast structures.

That dramatic delay of Etnachta by grouping parallel clause units (Judg 11:17) gives way in the next example to an ordinary clausal division based on a change in character (13:9). This verse also includes only two main actions and Etnachta stands between them (9a, b); the subsequent nominal clauses provide descriptive information.

Table 58. Division of clauses example: Judges 13:9

Action (God)	וַיִּשְׁמַע הָאֱלֹהִים בְּקוֹל מָנוֹחַ	9a
Action (Angel of God)	וַיָּבֹא מַלְאַךְ הָאֱלֹהִים עוֹד אֶל־הָאִשָּׁה	9b
NC (Mother) [break structure]	וְהִיא יוֹשֶׁבֶת בַּשָּׂדֶה	9c
NC (Father) [contrast]	וּמָנוֹחַ אִישָׁהּ אֵין עִמָּהּ:	9d

The contrast exists between these two nominal clauses (9c, d,). Both exhibit a break structure: the first stopping the forward action of the narrative (9c), the second to contrast with the content of the first nominal clause (9d). The major break in the second half-verse (9b–d) does not stand between the verbal clause (9b) and the first nominal clause (9c). Rather, the Zaqef stands between the contrasting clauses (9c, d). This indicates that while the Masoretes choose to prioritize dividing the verbal clauses with Etnachta, they still notice the contrast relationship and give it as much attention as possible.

This same principle, dividing the verbal clauses, occurs on an even smaller scale in Judges 20:42. Here the nominal clause (42b) comes between the two verbal clauses. The nominal clause offers a contrasting comment to the first verbal clause. The Masoretes, therefore, group these two clauses together in the Etnachta unit (cf. Judg 21:14 earlier in the chapter).

Table 59. Division of clauses example: Judges 20:42

Verbal Clause	וַיִּפְנ֞וּ לִפְנֵ֨י אִ֤ישׁ יִשְׂרָאֵל֙ אֶל־דֶּ֣רֶךְ הַמִּדְבָּ֔ר	42a
Nominal Clause [contrast]	וְהַמִּלְחָמָ֖ה הִדְבִּיקָ֑תְהוּ	42b
Verbal Clause	וַאֲשֶׁר֙ מֵהֶ֣עָרִ֔ים מַשְׁחִיתִ֥ים אוֹת֖וֹ בְּתוֹכֽוֹ׃	42c

If the nominal clause dropped out of the verse (42b), Etnachta would still reside in its most logical position, between the two verbal clauses. The contrast clause offers a very brief and passing comment in the midst of running narrative (42b). This may be why the Masoretes choose to group it with the first verbal clause, rather than highlight it with the major accent. Indeed, in all three of these foregoing examples, the

Masoretes make a choice to use the accents in a clausal manner, rather than highlight the contrast. Their choice comes down to clarity and simplicity in a verse that plays a rather minor role in the surrounding narrative.

Despite having to make choices between clausal grouping and highlighting contrast structures, these two features regularly collide at the same clausal juncture. In Judges 1:28, the Masoretes appropriately group the two lines of the temporal statement. Since the only remaining element in the verse is the contrast clause (28d), the main verse break falls between these two components. Thus, the most natural clause grouping and the point of contrast receive Etnachta.

Table 60. Division of clauses example: Judges 1:28

Intro to Event	וַיְהִי֙	28a
Temporal Clause	כִּֽי־חָזַ֣ק יִשְׂרָאֵ֔ל	28b
Result Clause	וַיָּ֥שֶׂם אֶת־הַֽכְּנַעֲנִ֖י לָמַ֑ס	28c
Contrast Structure	וְהוֹרֵ֖ישׁ לֹ֥א הוֹרִישֽׁוֹ׃ ס	28d

More clauses create more choices for accentuation. But in Judges 14:6, the most natural clause grouping and the point of contrast still occur at the same point. This text assembles around three main units: a preparatory action, a main action, and a contrast action. To protect Samson from the lion attack, the Spirit comes upon him (6a). This clause could potentially receive Etnachta but that would separate it from the act of ripping the lion to pieces (6b). Because these two acts must be viewed together, the Masoretes place a lower level accent between them.

Table 61. Division of clauses example: Judges 14:6

Preparatory Action	וַתִּצְלַח עָלָיו רוּחַ יְהוָה	6a
Main Action	וַיְשַׁסְּעֵ֫הוּ	6b
Comparison Clause	כְּשַׁסַּע הַגְּדִי	6c
Nominal Clause	וּמְאוּמָה אֵין בְּיָדוֹ	6d
Contrast Structure	וְלֹא הִגִּיד לְאָבִיו וּלְאִמּוֹ אֵת אֲשֶׁר עָשָׂה:	6e

It would also not make much sense to divide the comparison clause (6c) and the descriptive nominal clause (6d) from their head clause (6b). So that leaves one logical location for Etnachta, between the main actions of the verse and the contrastive commentary (6d). While it is possible that the contrast influenced the location of Etnachta in this verse (cf. Judg 14:9), it appear more likely that this location conveniently breaks the verse according clause groupings, which in this case also constitutes the point of contrast.

5.6   CONCLUSION

The Masoretic accentuation of contrast structures does not constitute an intentional pattern according to the strictures of this dissertation. Nevertheless, the Masoretes clearly intend to highlight contrast clauses with the strongest accent possible. Thus, when the contrast structure constitutes the main semantic feature in the surrounding text, this will often draw Etnachta (Judg 1:27; 2:17; 10:13) or a verse initial placement (Judg 7:25; 11:18; 14:9; 21:14). But due to the prevalence of other syntactic features (e.g., concluding mid-verse direct speech, framing conditional statements), other patterns often prevail over contrast structures for the major accent (Judg 15:13; 16:20). Likewise, a correct understanding of the verse may require the Masoretes to focus the reader on proper clausal groupings (Judg 11:17; 13:9; 20:42). Both prevailing patterns and clausal groups frequently intersect with the point of contrast (Judg 1:28; 2:2; 4:8; 14:6). So, while the Masoretic accentuation of contrast structures does not qualify as an intentional pattern, in certain cases it warrants their focused attention.

CHAPTER 6
CONCLUSION

6.1 INTRODUCTION

A desire to advance proper exegesis of the Hebrew Bible has propelled this thesis and course of inquiry. A love for God and his word leads naturally to a rigorous understanding of the biblical languages. Proper interpretive method begins with careful attention to the grammar, syntax, and vocabulary of the text. Vanhoozer writes,

> Language is a God-given capacity that enables human beings to relate to God, the world, and to one another. Specifically, language involves a kind of relating with God, the world, and others that yields personal knowledge. Language, that is, should be seen as the most important means and medium of communication and communion.... The proper function of our cognitive faculties, for instance, is to produce true belief. The proper function of our communicative faculties, I contend, is to produce true interpretation—understanding.[1]

An interpreter of any text must take language seriously. While the Masoretes are not infallible, they evince faithfulness and rigor in the interpretation they have provided to subsequent generations. Their work continues to demand careful analysis throughout the exegetical process.

The Masoretic accents clarify and confirm the sense of the text through predictable patterns. Their intentional divergence from these patterns indicates points of literary and semantic interest. The value of these regular patterns and divergent examples warrants greater attention

---

[1] Kevin J. Vanhoozer, *Is There a Meaning in this Text? The Bible, the Reader, and the Morality of Literary Knowledge* (Grand Rapids: Zondervan, 1998), 204–5.

by scholars and students. This dissertation examined four potential Masoretic accent patterns. Three patterns proved to be intentional patterns according to the standards laid out in this dissertation (the conclusion of mid-verse direct speech, the interjection ועתה, and framing conditional clauses). One did not meet the standard of an intentional pattern (contrast structures), nevertheless the Masoretes still pay this feature close attention.

6.2 REVIEW OF CASE STUDIES

Each chapter of this dissertation examined one syntactic feature to determine whether or not it constitutes an intentional Masoretic pattern. Chapter 2 presented the pattern for the conclusion of mid-verse direct speech. In the book of Judges, Etnachta concludes this feature 83 percent of the time (e.g., Judg 1:3; 4:9; 6:20; 7:9–11; 8:20; 15:1). The Masoretes occasionally diverge from this pattern for the sake of another semantic or syntactic feature that warrants greater prominence (e.g., Judg 11:38; 16:12; 16:30; 19:28). In each of these divergences, the end of direct speech receives the next strongest accent for the half-verse.

Chapter 3 examined the pattern for the interjection ועתה. From Genesis to Kings this strong lexical marker pairs with the strength of Etnachta 80 percent of the time (e.g., Judg 13:7; 15:18; 1 Sam 9:13; 2 Kgs 7:9). The Masoretes will depart from their pattern in order to (1) employ Etnachta on higher priority patterns (e.g., Gen 50:17; Josh 9:6,11; Judg 17:3; 18:14), (2) mark significant clause divisions (e.g., Gen 32:10; 2 Sam 24:10 and 1 Chr 21:8; 2 Sam 19:10–11), and (3) highlight semantic points on interest that occur in the same verse (e.g., Exod 3:18; Judg 6:13). Yet each case of divergence offers further evidence that the Masoretes intentionally place Etnachta before ועתה

whenever possible according to their pattern.

Chapter 4 opened up the pattern for framing conditional clauses: the subordinate accent concluding the protasis, the superior accent concluding the apodosis. This pattern defines conditionals 90 percent of the time in the book of Judges. The few examples that diverge from the stated pattern show a general conformity to the pattern once the complexity of their syntax unravels (e.g., Judg 6:36–37; 9:20: 21:21). A few examples from outside Judges demonstrate the ingenuity of the Masoretes in melding this pattern with other features of the text (e.g., Gen 13:9; Mal 1:6). Here again the pattern confirms and clarifies the sense of the text, all the while maintaining regular patterns.

Chapter 5 investigated the use of Masoretic accents in contexts of contrast, specifically in the presence of the contrast structures *vav* + X + verb, and *vav* + לא + verb. In the case of these structures, an intentional pattern did not present itself statistically, though the Masoretes clearly intend for contrast structures to receive attention. In other words, while these structures did not receive a consistent accentuation pattern due to the priority of other patterns and important clause divisions, the Masoretes highlight these structures when stronger syntactic and semantic influences do not intrude on the verse (e.g., Judg 1:27; 2:17; 7:25; 10:13; 11:18; 14:9; 21:14). This study illustrates the intentionality of the Masoretes to highlight the most important syntactic and semantic features of the verse, even though a singular accent pattern may not arise.

6.3   *IMPLICATIONS AND FUTURE STUDY*

At least three practical implications for exegesis develop out of this study: (1) accents assist in confirming clause boundaries to clarify the reading, (2) accents offer guidance in grouping clauses to better confirm the syntax, and (3) predictable accent patterns indicate points of literary interest.[2] The consistency and predictability of the accents benefits the interpreter in Bible reading. And the intentional divergence from these patterns often signals a point of semantic interest. But readers must know the typical patterns in order to spot divergence from them. These semantic signals often occur at transitions and conclusions (e.g., Judg 7:25; 9:20; 11:38; 16:30; 21:14), as well as around emphatic or surprising statements (e.g., Judg 6:13; 10:13; 19:28; 21:21). But this study only begins to open the door for more in-depth examinations of accent patterns.

The first path for future development begins with an exhaustive evaluation of all prose passages in the Hebrew Bible. This lack of comprehensive research represents a limitation of this dissertation in its present form, but the reader may judge if such a limitation was justified. Nevertheless, studying any one of these syntactic structures throughout all the prose passages of the Bible would secure the findings.

A second avenue for development takes a road through the rhetorical and literary structure of the writing prophets. The more vernacular prose of Judges allows for greater accentual variety. The prophetic and poetic compositions are more constricting due to the dominance of parallelism. But once some of these patterns become evident in prose, a study of their influence in more stylized texts would be worthwhile.

A third avenue for development would be to identify and examine other Masoretic accent patterns in the Hebrew Bible: question-

---

[2]Marcus Leman, "Reading with the Masoretes: The Exegetical Value of the Masoretic Accents," *Journal of Biblical and Theological Studies* 2 (Spring 2017): 42–51.

answer statements, temporal constructions ("when-then"), situation clauses, change of characters, vocatives, הנה clauses, and nominal versus verbal clauses. Some of these studies can be expected to parallel patterns uncovered in this dissertation (e.g., conditional statements and temporal constructions). Others may prove to be wild cards with unexpected results (e.g., הנה clauses).[3] With a full battery of Masoretic accent patterns, research may progress towards a logical hierarchy among these patterns.

6.4   *CONCLUSION*

The exiles had returned to the land, the temple had been rebuilt, the walls restored, the worship and priesthood reinstated. Then, on the first day of the seventh month, the people gathered in the open square. Ezra the scribe mounted a platform in the sight of all the people. He opened the Book of the Law and read in the hearing of all the people. Many other men were there as well to assist Ezra on this important occasion. "And they read in the book, in the Law of God, it being interpreted (פרש), and they gave the sense (שׂכל) so that the people understood (בין) the reading" (Neh 8:8). The Babylonian Talmud famously points to this dramatic event as encapsulating the modern synagogue traditions of reading the text with cantillation and Aramaic interpretation (*Meg.* 3a). Though the exact details of this day remain shrouded in the mists of time, this was a moving inception to a tradition that would stretch through the ages. The Masoretes believed they were guardians of that

---

[3]For example, in preparation of this dissertation I attempted a study of כי clauses and their various functions. My hypothesis was that כי subordinate clauses would follow a major accent like Etnachta. This ultimately proved an unfruitful study. Nevertheless, I did learn some of the characteristics that go into ch. 3 on ועתה, specifically the distinction of visible and invisible markers in the text.

tradition, and guarding required innovation in order to preserve their oral reading in written form. They were masters of the text longing for future generations to benefit from their mastery. Those who desire to exegete the text do well to hear their voice and read with the Masoretes.

APPENDIX 1
MASORETIC ACCENT HIERARCHY

Table A1. Transliteration of the *te'amim*

From the כ"א (Book of the 21)		*From the* אמ"ת (Book of the 3)	
סוֹף פָּסוּק׃	Sof Pasuq	עוֹלֶה־וְיוֹרֵד	Oleh Veyored
סִלּוּק	Siluq	רְבִיעַ (מוּגְרָשׁ)	Revia (Mugrash)
אֶתְנַחְתָּא	Etnachta	שַׁלְשֶׁלֶת גְּדוֹלָה ׀	Shalshelet Gedolah
טִפְחָא	Tipecha	צִינּוֹר	Tsinor
זָקֵף (־גָּדוֹל)	Zaqef (Gadol)	דֶּחִי	Dechi
סֶגוֹל	Segol	מַהְפָּךְ לְגַרְמֵהּ ׀	Mahpakh Legarmeh
תְּבִיר	Tevir	אַזְלָא לְגַרְמֵהּ ׀	Azla Legarmeh
פַּשְׁטָא [יְתִיב]	Pashta [Yetiv]	עִלּוּי	Iluy
זַרְקָא	Zarqa	טַרְחָא	Tarchah
רְבִיעַ	Revia	שַׁלְשֶׁלֶת קְטַנָּה	Shalshelet Qetanah
גֶּרֶשׁ (גֵּרְשַׁיִם)	Geresh (Gereshayim)	צִינּוֹרִית	Tsinorit

151

לְגַרְמֵהּ ׀	Legarmeh	אַזְלָא	Azla
תְּלִישָׁה־גְדוֹלָה	Telishah Gedolah	מֵרְכָא מְצוּנָּר	Merekha Metsunar
פָּזֵר (־גָּדוֹל)	Pazer (Gadol)	מַהְפַּךְ מְצוּנָּר	Mahpakh Metsunar
שַׁלְשֶׁלֶת ׀	Shalshelet	Other Signs	
מוּנַח	Munach	מֶתֶג	Meteg
מֵרְכָא (־כְּפוּלָה)	Merekha (Khefulah)	מָאיְלָא	Ma'yela
קַדְמָה	Qadmah	מְתִיגָה־זָקֵף	Metigah-Zaqef
מַהְפַּךְ	Mahpakh	מַקֵּף־	Maqef
דַּרְגָּא	Darga	פָּסֵק ׀	Paseq
תְּלִישָׁה־קְטַנָּה	Telishah Qetanah		
גַּלְגַּל	Galgal		

Notes:
1) These accent names are taken from Jacobson's *Chanting the Hebrew Bible*. They represent a consistent Ashkenazi list of names. For a comparison of Sephardic and Ashkenazi names see Buth, *Living Biblical Hebrew ב: Selected Readings*, 115–22. Note that Sof Pasuq is not an accent but is part of the hierarchy.
2) Transliterations are for basic English pronunciation purposes. This conforms to the SBL General Purpose transliteration style, though spirants not spoken in modern dialects have been omitted.

Table A2. Accent hierarchy for the 21 books

Conjunctive and Disjunctive Accents (21 Books)					
Far	Near	Rank	Symbol	Conjunctives	Disjunctives
Etnachta	Siluq	(Emperor)	דבר:	[o]	Sof Pasuq
					Kings
Zaqef	Tipecha	Near King	דָּבָר	מירכָא	Siluq
Zaqef/Segol	Tipecha	Far King	דָּבָר	מוּנַח	Etnachta
					Princes
Revia	Tevir	Near Prince	דָּבָר	מירכָא	Tipecha
Revia	Pashta	Far Prince	דָּבָר דָּבָר	מוּנַח	Zaqef (Gadol)
Revia	Zarqa	Far Prince	דָּבָר	מוּנַח	Segol (‵)
					Dukes
Telisha/Pazer	Geresh	Near Duke	דָּבָר	מוּנַח תְּלִישָׁה קַדְמָה דַּרְגָּא (מירכָא)‵	Tevir
Telisha/Pazer	Geresh	Near Duke	דְּבַר מֶלֶךְ	מוּנַח תְּלִישָׁה קַדְמָה מירכָא // קַדְמָה (מוּנַח)‵ מהפָּךְ (מירכָא)‵	Pashta (‵) Yetiv (′)
Telisha/Pazer	Geresh	Near Duke	דָּבָר	מוּנַח תְּלִישָׁה קַדְמָה מוּנַח (מירכָא)‵	Zarqa (‵)
Telisha/Pazer	Geresh	Far Duke	דָּבָר	מוּנַח דַּרְגָּא מוּנַח	Revia
Conjunctives					Counts
Munach (דָּבָר)		Near Count	דָּבָר דָּבָר	מוּנַח תְּלִישָׁה קַדְמָה (מוּנַח)‵ [מוּנַח]	Geresh [Gereshayim]
Merekha (דָּבָר)		Near Count	דָּבָר ׀	מירכָא	Legarmeh
Merekha Khefulah (דָּבָר)		Far Count	דבר	מוּנַח	Telishah Gedolah (′)
Qadmah (דָּבָר)		Far Count	דָּבָר	מוּנַח	Pazer
Mahpakh (דָּבָר)		Far Count	דָּבָר	מוּנַח גַּלְגַּל	Pazer Gadol
Darga (דָּבָר)					Others
Telishah Qetanah (דָּבָר)			מֶלֶךְ	(See Pashta)	Terey-Qadmiyn
Galgal (דָּבָר)			דָּבָר ׀	(See Segol)	Shalshelet

*The parenthetical accent may replace the accent immediately before it. ◊ (′) prepositive // (‵) postpositive position

Sources: James D. Price adapted by Russell Fuller (*Invitation to Biblical Hebrew Syntax*), William Wickes (*Treatise on the Accentuation of the Twenty-One*), Joshua R. Jacobson (*Chanting the Hebrew Bible*)

Table A2 depicts the accent hierarchy according to a five tiered system. To translate this table into a four tiered system simply collapse the top category (Emperor, קיסר) into the second tier (Kings, מלכים) or ignore it entirely. Each rank includes the name of the disjunctive accent, common preceding conjunctives, the symbol for the accent, its standing as a subordinate, and the accents directly subordinate to its domain. For the conjunctive accents, only the name and a basic translation are provided. Read the conjunctives in order from right to left. The entire string of conjunctives will not always precede the disjunctive.

The main value of this chart is its depiction of the various ranks, relationships, and their near/far subordinates. In order to provide all this information in such a small space, certain complex issues have been simplified. For the fullest explanation of accent rules and relationships, see the extended works by Wickes, Fuller, and Jacobson listed in the bibliography. For a similar chart, see Russell T. Fuller and Kyoungwon Choi, *Invitation to Biblical Hebrew Syntax: An Intermediate Grammar* (Grand Rapids: Kregel, 2016), Accents §2.B–C.

APPENDIX 2
TEXT CRITICAL WORK: JUDGES 16:13

Table A3. Ancient translations of Judges 16:13

Hebrew (MT)	16:13 וַתֹּאמֶר דְּלִילָה אֶל־שִׁמְשׁוֹן עַד־הֵנָּה הֵתַלְתָּ בִּי וַתְּדַבֵּר אֵלַי כְּזָבִים הַגִּידָה לִּי בַּמֶּה תֵּאָסֵר וַיֹּאמֶר אֵלֶיהָ אִם־תַּאַרְגִי אֶת־שֶׁבַע מַחְלְפוֹת רֹאשִׁי עִם־הַמַּסָּכֶת: 16:14 וַתִּתְקַע בַּיָּתֵד וַתֹּאמֶר אֵלָיו פְּלִשְׁתִּים עָלֶיךָ שִׁמְשׁוֹן וַיִּיקַץ מִשְּׁנָתוֹ וַיִּסַּע אֶת־הַיְתַד הָאֶרֶג וְאֶת־הַמַּסָּכֶת:
Hebrew (DSS)	(not extant)
Hebrew (medieval variants)	(no consequential variants in Kennicott or de Rossi)
Greek (LXX-A)	16:13 καὶ εἶπεν Δαλιλα πρὸς Σαμψων Ἕως νῦν παρελογίσω με καὶ ἐλάλησας πρός με ψευδῆ· ἀνάγγειλον δή μοι ἐν τίνι δεθήσῃ. <u>καὶ εἶπεν πρὸς αὐτήν Ἐὰν ὑφάνῃς τὰς ἑπτὰ σειρὰς τῆς κεφαλῆς μου μετὰ τοῦ διάσματος</u> καὶ ἐγκρούσῃς ἐν τῷ πασσάλῳ εἰς τὸν τοῖχον, καὶ ἔσομαι ἀσθενὴς ὡς εἷς τῶν ἀνθρώπων. 16:14 καὶ ἐκοίμισεν αὐτὸν Δαλιλα καὶ ἐδιάσατο τοὺς ἑπτὰ βοστρύχους τῆς κεφαλῆς αὐτοῦ μετὰ τῆς ἐκτάσεως <u>καὶ κατέκρουσεν ἐν τοῖς πασσάλοις</u> εἰς τὸν τοῖχον καὶ εἶπεν πρὸς αὐτόν Οἱ ἀλλόφυλοι ἐπὶ σέ, Σαμψων· καὶ ἐξηγέρθη ἐκ τοῦ ὕπνου αὐτοῦ καὶ ἐξέσπασεν τοὺς πασσάλους σὺν τῷ ὑφάσματι ἐκ τοῦ τοίχου καὶ τὸ δίασμα, καὶ οὐκ ἐγνώσθη ἡ ἰσχὺς αὐτοῦ.

Table A3 continued

Greek (LXX-B)	16:13 καὶ εἶπεν Δαλιδα πρὸς Σαμψων Ἰδοὺ ἐπλάνησάς με καὶ ἐλάλησας πρὸς ἐμὲ ψευδῆ· ἀπάγγειλον δή μοι ἐν τίνι δεθήσῃ. <u>καὶ εἶπεν πρὸς αὐτήν Ἐὰν ὑφάνῃς τὰς ἑπτὰ σειρὰς τῆς κεφαλῆς μου σὺν τῷ διάσματι</u> καὶ ἐγκρούσῃς τῷ πασσάλῳ εἰς τὸν τοῖχον, καὶ ἔσομαι ὡς εἷς τῶν ἀνθρώπων ἀσθενής. 16:14 καὶ ἐγένετο ἐν τῷ κοιμᾶσθαι αὐτὸν καὶ ἔλαβεν Δαλιδα τὰς ἑπτὰ σειρὰς τῆς κεφαλῆς αὐτοῦ καὶ ὕφανεν ἐν τῷ διάσματι καὶ <u>ἔπηξεν τῷ πασσάλῳ</u> εἰς τὸν τοῖχον καὶ εἶπεν Ἀλλόφυλοι ἐπὶ σέ, Σαμψων· καὶ ἐξυπνίσθη ἐκ τοῦ ὕπνου αὐτοῦ καὶ ἐξῆρεν τὸν πάσσαλον τοῦ ὑφάσματος ἐκ τοῦ τοίχου.
Greek (Hexapla)	(no consequential variants)
Aramaic (Targum)	16:13 וַאֲמַרַת דְּלִילָה לְשִׁמְשׁוֹן עַד הָכָא שַׁקַּרְתְּ בִּי וּמַלֵּילְתְּ עִמִּי כַּדְבִין חַוִּי לִי בְּמָא תִתְאֲסַר <u>וַאֲמַר לַהּ אִם תֶּשְׁתֵּן יָת שְׁבַע גְּדִילַת רֵישִׁי עִם אַכְסְנָא בְּמַשְׁתִּיתָא</u>: 16:14 וּנְקֻשַׁת בְּסִכְּתָא וַאֲמַרַת לֵיהּ פְּלִשְׁתָּאֵי אֲתוֹ עֲלָךְ שִׁמְשׁוֹן וְאִתְעַר מִשְׁנָתֵיהּ וּנְטַל יָת אַכְסַן דְּגַרְדְּיָאִין וְיָת מַשְׁתִּיתָא:
Syriac (Peshitta)	16:13 ܘܐܡܪܬ ܕܠܝܠܐ ܠܫܡܫܘܢ ܗܐ ܓܚܟܬ ܒܝ ܘܐܡܪܬ ܠܝ ܕܓܠܬܐ ܚܘܐ ܠܝ ܒܡܢܐ ܬܬܐܣܪ. ܘܐܡܪ ܠܗ ܐܢ ܬܐܙܠܝܢ ܫܒܥ ܓܕܠܬܐ ܕܪܝܫܝ ܥܡ ܡܫܬܝܬܐ. 16:14 ܘܐܬܩܢܬ ܒܣܟܬܐ ܘܐܡܪܬ ܠܗ ܦܠܫܬܝܐ ܐܬܘ ܥܠܝܟ ܫܡܫܘܢ. ܘܐܬܬܥܝܪ ܡܢ ܫܢܬܗ ܘܫܩܠ ܠܣܟܬܐ ܕܓܪܕܝܐ ܘܠܡܫܬܝܬܐ.
Latin (Old Latin)	(not extant)[1]

---

[1] Butler includes a translation of Old Latin, "If you take apart the seven locks of my head and you lay the warp of a web and you lay bare my hairs in it as if the web is covered over, I will become weak. And Delilah made him sleep and she took apart

Table A3 continued

Latin (Vulgate)	16:13 dixitque Dalila rursum ad eum usquequo decipis me et falsum <u>loqueris ostende quo vinciri debeas si inquit septem crines capitis mei cum licio plexueris</u> et clavum his circumligatum terrae fixeris infirmus ero 16:14 quod cum fecisset Dalila dixit ad eum Philisthim super te Samson qui consurgens de somno extraxit clavum cum crinibus et licio

External Evidence—Two main readings present themselves: (1) the shorter of the MT, and (2) the longer of the LXX. The Aramaic and Syriac follow the MT reading and medieval Hebrew manuscripts only show variants in the minutiae. The Latin Vulgate offers a longer reading, but Jerome appears to have translated more freely and shorter than the full LXX reading. It remains possible that Jerome may have had a shorter manuscript and inserted this line to complete the conditional based on the complete lines in Judges 16:7, 11. More likely Jerome has shortened his reading from one of the LXX renderings.

Internal Evidence—The longer reading makes better sense of the context and avoids an awkward skip from 16:13 to 16:14, "'If you weave seven locks of my head with a loom' ... and she tightened with a peg" (MT). The longer reading both completes the conditional and the context of Samson's instructions, "'If you weave the seven lengths of my head with a loom [and fasten (them) with a peg into the wall, then I will be as one of the weak men.' And it happened when he went to sleep

---

the seven hears of his head with fear, and she went out in the length of the room, and she fixed it in pins and she said to him ..." (Judg 16:13b–14a). Trent C. Butler, *Judges*, WBC 8 (Nashville: Thomas Nelson, 2009), 316. He does not present the origin of this translation in his commentary. *Bibliorum Sacrorum Latinæ versiones antiquæ* (Sabatier, 1743) does not contain this reading.

that Delilah took the seven lengths of his head and wove (them) into the loom] and fastened them with a peg into the wall" (LXX-B).² The missing bracketed portion both completes the spoken conditional and re-establishes the context for the resumption of narrative.

Summary Conclusion—The internal evidence suggests that in this case the LXX has preserved the original reading. Despite the fact that the MT offers the more difficult reading, its difficulties seem explainable as a scribal error. While the reader of the MT might be able to infer the conclusion of the conditional from previous verses (16:7, 11), the re-establishment of narrative context does not occur in the MT reading. Further, the rather literal translation of LXX-B offers a clue as to what error may have occurred in the manuscript tradition. The repetition of the phrase τῷ διάσματι καὶ in both verses show that this may have led to a simple case of haplography in the Hebrew transmission. Reconstruction of the *Vorlage* of LXX-B yields the necessary text to arrive at עם המסכת ותתקע ביתד. Thus, a scribe prior to the time of the Masoretes likely skipped from one occurrence of המסכת to the next causing the omission.³

---

²The comment about "into the wall" seems to be movement from the general literal style of LXX-B to a more interpretive comment (cf. the Latin translation(s)).

³Daniel I. Block, *Judges, Ruth,* NAC 6 (Nashville: B&H, 1999), 458; Butler, *Judges*, 316; Natalio Fernández Marcos, *Judges*, Biblia Hebraica Quinta 7 (Stuttgart: Deutsche Bibelgesellschaft, 2011), 96*–97*.

Bibliography

Alexander, Philip S. "How Did the Rabbis Learn Hebrew?" Pages 71–89 in *Hebrew Study From Ezra to Ben-Yehuda*. Edited by William Hornbury. Edinburgh: T&T Clark, 1999.

Arnold, Bill T., and John H. Choi. *A Guide to Biblical Hebrew Syntax*. New York: Cambridge University Press, 2003.

Baker, David W. "Scribes as Transmitters of Tradition." Pages 65–78 in *Faith, Tradition, and History: Old Testament Historiography in Its Near Eastern Context*. Edited by A. R. Millard, James K. Hoffmeier, and David W. Baker. Winona Lake, IN: Eisenbrauns, 1994.

Barthélemy, Dominique. *Critique Textuelle de l'Ancien Testament*. Vol. 1. Fribourg, Switzerland: Éditions Universitaires Fribourg/Suisse, 1982.

———. *Studies in the Text of the Old Testament: An Introduction to the Hebrew Old Testament Text Project*. Translated by Sarah Lind. Vol. 3 of *Textual Criticism and the Translator*. Winona Lake, IN: Eisenbrauns, 2012.

Beckman, John C. "Conditional Clause: Biblical Hebrew." In vol. 1 of *Encyclopedia of Hebrew Language and Linguistics*, 545–48. Boston: Brill, 2013.

Ben-Asher, Aharon. *The Diqduqe Hate'amim of Aharon Ben Moshe Ben Asher: With a Critical Edition of the Original Text from New Manuscripts*. Edited by Aron Dotan. Jerusalem: Academy of the Hebrew Language, 1967.

Binder, Abraham W. *Biblical Chant*. New York: Sacred Music Press, 1959.

Block, Daniel I. *Judges, Ruth*. NAC 6. Nashville: B&H, 1999.

Breuer, Mordecai. פיסוק טעמים שבמקרא: תורת דקדוק הטעמים. Jerusalem: World Zionist Organization (ההסתדרות הציונית), 1958.

Brown, Francis, Samuel R. Driver, and Charles A. Briggs. *The Brown-Driver-Briggs Hebrew and English Lexicon*. Peabody, MA: Hendrickson, 2012.

Buth, Randall. "Functional Grammar, Hebrew and Aramaic: An Integrated Textlinguistic Approach to Syntax." Pages 77–102 in *Discourse Analysis of Biblical Literature: What It Is, and What It Offers*. Edited by Walter J. Bodine. Atlanta: Scholars Press, 1995.

———. *Living Biblical Hebrew ב: Selected Readings with 500 Friends*. Jerusalem: Biblical Language Center, 2006.

Butler, Trent C. *Judges*. WBC 8. Nashville: Thomas Nelson, 2009.

Celce-Murcia, Marianne, and Diane Larsen-Freeman. *The Grammar Book: An ESL/EFL Teacher's Course*. Boston: Heinle-Cengage Learning, 1999.

Cohen, Miles B. *The System of Accentuation in the Hebrew Bible*. Minneapolis: Milco Press, 1969.

Davies, Philip R. "Biblical Hebrew and the History of Ancient Judah: Typology, Chronology and Common Sense." Pages 150–63 in *Biblical Hebrew*. Edited by Ian Young. New York: T&T Clark, 2003.

De Hoop, Raymond. "Isaiah 40.13, the Masoretes, Syntax, and Literary Structure: A Rejoinder to Reinoud Oosting." *JSOT* 33 (2009): 453–63.

Dotan, Aron, ed. *Biblia Hebraica Leningradensia: Prepared According to the Vocalization, Accents, and Masora of Aaron Ben Moses Ben Asher in the Leningrad Codex*. Peabody, MA: Henrickson, 2001.

———. "Masorah." Pages 603–56 in vol. 13 of *Encyclopedia Judaica*. Edited by Fred Skolnik and Michael Berenbaum. New York: Macmillan Reference, 2007.

———. "The Relative Chronology of Hebrew Vocalization and Accentuation." *Proceedings of the American Academy for Jewish Research* 48 (1981): 87–99.

Dresher, Bezalel Elan. "Biblical Accents: Prosody." Pages 288–96 in vol. 1 of *Encyclopedia of Hebrew Language and Linguistics*. Edited by Geoffrey Khan. Boston: Brill, 2013.

———. "The Prosodic Basis of the Tiberian System of Hebrew Accents." *Language* 70 (1994): 1–52.

Driver, Samuel R. *A Treatise on the Use of the Tenses in Hebrew and Some Other Syntactical Questions*. Oxford University Press, 1892. Reprint, Eugene, OR: Wipf and Stock, 2004.

Elliger, Karl, William Rudolph, and Adrian Schenker, eds. *Biblia Hebraica Stuttgartensia*. Stuttgart: Deutsche Bibelgesellschaft, 1983.

Freedman, David B., and Miles B. Cohen. "The Masoretes as Exegetes: Selected Examples." Pages 35–46 in *1972 and 1973 Proceedings IOMS*. Edited by Harry M. Orlinsky. Missoula, MT: Scholars Press, 1974.

Fuller, Russell T. "John Owen and the Traditional Protestant View of the Hebrew Old Testament." *The Southern Baptist Journal of Theology* 20 (2016): 79–99.

Fuller, Russell T., and Kyoungwon Choi. *Invitation to Biblical Hebrew: A Beginning Grammar*. Grand Rapids: Kregel, 2006.

———. *Invitation to Biblical Hebrew Syntax: An Intermediate Grammar*. Grand Rapids: Kregel, 2016.

Garrett, Duane A. *Rethinking Genesis: Sources and Authorship for the First Book of the Pentateuch*. Grand Rapids: Baker, 1991.

Garrett, Duane A., and Jason S. DeRouchie. *A Modern Grammar for Biblical Hebrew*. Nashville: B&H, 2009.

Goshen-Gottstein, Moshe H. "The Aleppo Codex and the Rise of the Massoretic Bible Text." *The Biblical Archaeologist* 42 (Summer 1979): 145–63.

———. "The Authenticity of the Aleppo Codex." Pages 17–58 in *Text and Language in Bible and Qumran*. Jerusalem: Orient, 1960.

———. "The Rise of the Tiberian Bible Text." Pages 79–122 in *Biblical and Other Studies*. Edited by Alexander Altmann. Cambridge: Harvard University Press, 1963.

Hanau, Shlomo. שערי זמרה הארוך. Brooklyn, NY: Rabbi Y. A. Guttman, 2003.

Hornkohl, Aaron. "The Pragmatics of the X-Verb Structure in the Hebrew of Genesis: The Linguistic Functions and Associated Effects and Meanings of Intra-Clausal Fronted Constituents." M.A. thesis, Hebrew University, 2003.

Jacobson, Joshua. "Cantillation of the Psalms." *Journal of Synagogue Music* 39 (2014): 17–34.

———. *Chanting the Hebrew Bible: The Art of Cantillation*. Philadelphia: Jewish Publication Society, 2002.

———. *Chanting the Hebrew Bible: Student Edition*. Philadelphia: Jewish Publication Society, 2005.

———. "Sometimes a Munah Pasek is Just a Munah Pasek." *Journal of Synagogue Music* 42 (2017): 17–34.

Janis, Norman. "A Grammar of the Biblical Accents." PhD diss., Harvard University, 1987.

Kaiser, Walter C., Jr., and Moisés Silva. *An Introduction to Biblical Hermeneutics: The Search for Meaning*. Grand Rapids: Zondervan, 1994.

Kelley, Page H., Daniel S. Mynatt, and Timothy G. Crawford. *The Masorah of Biblia Hebraica Stutthartensia: Introduction and Annotated Glossary*. Grand Rapids: Eerdmans, 1998.

Khan, Geoffrey. *The Early Karaite Tradition of Hebrew Grammatical Thought*. Boston: Brill, 2000.

———. *A Short Introduction to the Tiberian Masoretic Bible and Its Reading Tradition*. Vol. 25 of Gorgias Handbooks. Edited by George Anton Kiraz. Piscataway, NJ: Gorgias, 2012.

Koehler, Ludwig, and Walter Baumgartner. *The Hebrew and Aramaic Lexicon of the Old Testament*. Electronic ed. Translated by M. E. J. Richardson. Altamonte Springs, FL: OakTree Software, 2000.

Kutscher, Eduard Yechezkel. *A History of the Hebrew Language*. Leiden: Brill, 1982.

LaSor, William S. "An Approach to Hebrew Poetry Through the Masoretic Accents." Pages 327–53 in *Essays on the Occasion of the Seventieth Anniversary of the Dropsie University*. Edited by Abraham I. Katsh, and Leon Nemoy. Philadelphia: The Dropsie University, 1979.

Leman, Marcus A. "Reading With the Masoretes: The Exegetical Value of the Masoretic Accents." *Journal of Biblical and Theological Studies* 2 (2017): 42–51.

Lode, Lars. "A Discourse Perspective on the Significance of the Masoretic Accents." Pages 155–74 in *Biblical Hebrew and Discourse Linguistics*. Edited by Robert D. Bergen. Dallas: Summer Institute of Linguistics, 1994.

Marcos, Natalio Fernández. "The Hebrew and Greek Texts of Judges." Pages 1–16 in *The Earliest Text of the Hebrew Bible: The Relationship between the Masoretic Text and the Hebrew Base of the Septuagint Reconsidered*, edited by Adrian Schenker. Atlanta: Society of Biblical Literature, 2003.

———. *Judges*. Biblia Hebraica Quinta 7. Stuttgart: Deutsche Bibelgesellschaft, 2011.

Mashiah, Rachel. "Parallel Divisional Patterns in Biblical Accentuation in the Twenty-One Prose Books, According to the Leningrad Codex." PhD diss., Bar-Ilan University, 1995.

———. "Parallel Realizations of Dichotomy Patterns in Biblical Accentuation." Pages 59–69 in *Proceedings of the Twelfth International Congress of the International Organization for Masoretic Studies*. Edited by E. J. Revell. Atlanta: Scholars Press, 1996.

McDonald, Richard Charles. "Grammatical Analysis of Various Biblical Hebrew Texts According to Traditional Semitic Grammar." PhD diss., The Southern Baptist Theological Seminary, 2014.

McEnery, Tony, and Andrew Hardie. *Corpus Linguistics: Method, Theory and Practice*. New York: Cambridge, 2012.

Miller, Cynthia. *The Representation of Speech in Biblical Hebrew Narrative: A Linguistic Analysis*. HSM 55. Edited by Peter Machinist. Atlanta: Scholars Press, 1996.

Moshavi, Adina M. *Word Order in the Biblical Hebrew Finite Clause: A Syntactic and Pragmatic Analysis of Preposing*. Linguistic Studies in Ancient West Semitic 4. Winona Lake, IN: Eisenbrauns, 2010.

Niccacci, Alviero. "Result Clause: Biblical Hebrew." Pages 390–94 in vol. 3 of *Encyclopedia of Hebrew Language and Linguistics*. Edited by Geoffrey Khan. Brill, Boston, 2013.

Ofer, Yosef. "The History and Authority of the Aleppo Codex." Pages 25–50 in *Jerusalem Crown: Companion Volume*. Edited by Mordechai Glatzer. Jerusalem: N. Ben-Zvi Printing, 2002.

Olszowy-Schlanger, Judith. "The Knowledge of Hebrew among Early Karaites, and Its Use in Karaite Legal Contracts." Pages 165–85 in *Hebrew Study From Ezra to Ben-Yehuda*. Edited by William Hornbury. Edinburgh: T&T Clark, 1999.

Park, Sung Jin. "'Pointing to the Accents in the Scroll': Functional Development of the Masoretic Accents in the Hebrew Bible." *Hebrew Studies* 55 (2014): 73–88.

Patmore, Hector M. "Did the Masoretes Get it Wrong? The Vocalization and Accentuation of Ezekiel Xxviii 12–19." *Vetus Testamentum* 58 (2008): 245–57.

Perlman, Michael. *Dappim Lelimud Ta'Amey Ha-Mikra*. Jerusalem: Hamakhon Ha-Yisra'eli Lemusikah Datit, 1962.

———. ספר במדבר. Tel Aviv: Zimrat, 1981.

———. ספר בראשית. Tel Aviv: Zimrat, 1979.

———. ספר דברים. Tel Aviv: Zimrat, 1981.

———. ספר ההפטרות. Tel Aviv: Zimrat, 1987.

———. ספר ויקרא. Tel Aviv: Zimrat, 1980.

———. ספר יהושע. Tel Aviv: Zimrat, 1984.

———. ספר שמות. Tel Aviv: Zimrat, 1981.

———. ספר תהלים. Tel Aviv: Zimrat, 1982.

Praetorius, Franz. *Über Die Herkunft Der Hebräischen Accente*. New York: Lemcke & Buechner, 1901.

Price, James D. *Concordance of the Hebrew Accents in the Hebrew Bible*. Studies in the Bible and Early Christianity 34. Lewiston, NY: Mellen, 1996.

———. *The Syntax of Masoretic Accents in the Hebrew Bible*. Studies in the Bible and Early Christianity 27. Lewiston, NY: Mellen, 1990.

Revell, E. J. *Biblical Texts with Palestinian Pointing and Their Accents*. MasS 4. Missoula, MT: Scholars Press, 1977.

———. *Nesiga (Retraction of Word Stress) in Tiberian Hebrew*. Madrid: Instituto de Filologia, C.S.I.C., 1987.

———. "Pausal Forms in Biblical Hebrew: Their Function, Origin, and Significance." *Journal of Semitic Studies* 25 (1980): 165–79.

———. *The Pausal System: Divisions in the Hebrew Biblical Text as Marked by Voweling and Stress Position*. Vol. 10 of Pericope. Edited by Raymond de Hoop, and Paul Sanders. Sheffield: Sheffield Phoenix, 2015.

Rubin, Aaron D. "Samuel Archivolti and the Antiquity of the Hebrew Pointing." *The Jewish Quarterly Review* 101 (2011): 233–43.

Sáenz-Badillos, Angel. *A History of the Hebrew Language*. Translated by John Elwolde. New York: Cambridge University Press, 1993.

Segal, Michael, Emanuel Tov, William B. Seales, Clifford S. Parker, Pnina Shor, Yosef Porath, and Ada Yardeni. "An Early Leviticus Scroll From En-Gedi: Preliminary Publication." *Textus* 26, (2016): 1–30.

Smelik, Willem F. "Orality, Manuscript Reproduction, and the Targums." Pages 49–81 in *Paratext and Megatext as Channels of Jewish and Christian Traditions: The Textual Markers of Contextualization*. Edited by August den Hollander, Ulrich Schmid, and Willem Smelik. Boston: Brill, 2003.

Spanier, Arthur. *Die Massoretischen Akzente—Eine Darlegung Ihres Systems Nebst Beiträgen zum Verständnis Ihrer Entwicklung*. Berlin: Akademie-Verlag, 1927.

Stec, David, Siam Bhayro, Jacqueline C. R. de Roo, and Helen Spurling. "עַתָּה." Pages 633–39 in vol. 6 of *The Dictionary of Classical Hebrew*. Edited by David J. A. Clines. Sheffield, England: Sheffield Phoenix, 2007.

Steiner, Richard C. "Does the Biblical Hebrew Conjunction -ו Have Many Meanings, One Meaning, or No Meaning at All?" *JBL* 119, (2000): 249–67.

van der Merwe, Christo H. J., Jackie A. Naudé, and Jan H. Kroeze. *A Biblical Hebrew Reference Grammar*. Edited by Stanley E. Porter, and Richard S. Hess. Sheffield, England: Sheffield Academic, 1999.

Vanhoozer, Kevin J. *Is There a Meaning in This Text? The Bible, the Reader, and the Morality of Literary Knowledge*. Grand Rapids: Zondervan, 1998.

Walker, Helen M., and Joseph Lev. *Elementary Statistical Methods*. Rev. ed. New York: Holt, Rinehart and Winston, 1958.

Waltke, Bruce K., and Michael P. O'Connor. *An Introduction to Biblical Hebrew Syntax*. Winona Lake, IN: Eisenbrauns, 1990.

Weil, Daniel M. *The Masoretic Chant of the Bible*. Jerusalem: Rubin Mass, 1995.

Wickes, William. "A Treatise on the Accentuation of the Three So-Called Poetical Books of the Old Testment, Psalms, Proverbs, and Job (טעמי אמ״ת)." Vol. 1 of *Two Treatises on the Accentuation of the Old Testament*, edited by Harry M. Orlinsky. New York: KTAV, 1970.

―――――. "A Treatise on the Accentuation of the Twenty-One So-Called Prose Books of the Old Testament (טעמי כ״א ספרים)." Vol. 2 of *Two Treatises on the Accentuation of the Old Testament*, edited by Harry M. Orlinsky. New York: KTAV, 1970.

Williams, Frederick. *Reasoning With Statistics: How to Read Quantitative Research*. 3rd ed. New York: Holt, Rinehart and Winston, 1986.

Williams, Ronald J. *Williams' Hebrew Syntax*. 3rd ed. Edited by John C. Beckman. Toronto: University of Toronto Press, 2007.

Würthwein, Ernst. *The Text of the Old Testament: An Introduction to the Biblia Hebraica*, 3rd Edition. Translated by Erroll F. Rhodes. Grand Rapids: Eerdmans, 2014.

Yeivin, Israel. *Introduction to the Tiberian Masorah*. Translated by E. J. Revell. Missoula, MT: Scholars Press, 1980.

Author Index

Arnold, Bill T., *53, 60, 79, 116, 159*
Barthélemy, Dominique, *11, 17, 104, 159*
Beckman, John C., *79, 159, 167*
Ben-Asher, Aharon, *22, 159*
Bhayro, Siam, *53, 166*
Binder, Abraham W., *9, 159*
Block, Daniel I., *73, 102, 132, 134, 158, 159*
Breuer, Mordecai, *20-22, 30, 159*
Buth, Randall, *3, 53-54, 115-17, 152, 160*
Butler, Trent C., *134, 156, 158, 160*
Celce-Murcia and Larsen-Freeman, *114, 160*
Choi, John H., *53, 60, 79, 116, 159*
Choi, Kyoungwon, *3, 11, 13, 21, 25, 32, 34, 38, 48, 50, 57-58, 61, 69, 71, 79-80, 83, 85, 100, 110, 115-18, 132, 135, 154, 161*
Cohen, Miles B., *21-22, 160-61*

de Roo, Jacqueline C. R., *53, 166*
DeRouchie, Jason S., *x, 38, 87, 115, 161*
Dotan, Aron, *16-19, 22-23, 27, 105, 159-60*
Dresher, Bezalel Elan, *10, 26, 29-30, 107, 109, 161*
Driver, Samuel R., *5, 113-14, 160-61*
Fuller, Russell T., *x, 3, 11, 13, 21, 25, 31-32, 34, 38, 48, 50, 57-58, 61, 69, 71, 79-80, 83, 85, 100, 110, 115-18, 132, 135, 154, 161*
Garrett, Duane A., *38, 47, 87, 115, 161*
Goshen-Gottstein, Moshe H., *20-21, 161-62*
Hanau, Shlomo, *17-18, 162*
Hardie, Andrew, *6, 164*
Hornkohl, Aaron, *116-17, 127, 162*
Jacobson, Joshua, *3, 9-10, 13, 15, 30, 34, 38, 50,*

70-71, 84-85, 89, 106-7, 117, 152, 154, 162
Janis, Norman, *10, 27-28, 109, 162*
Khan, Geoffrey, *3, 21, 26, 105, 161-62, 164*
Kroeze, Jan H., *54, 79, 166*
Kutscher, Eduard Yechezkel, *14, 163*
Leman, Marcus A., *148, 163*
Lode, Lars, *4, 163*
Marcos, Natalio Fernández, *102-3, 158, 163*
Mashiah, Rachel, *26-27, 163*
McDonald, Richard Charles, *71, 164*
McEnery, Tony, *6, 164*
Miller, Cynthia, *71, 164*
Moshavi, Adina M., *116-17, 164*
Naudé, Jackie A., *54, 79, 166*
O'Connor, Michael P., *53, 71, 79, 166*
Ofer, Yosef, *12, 14-16, 21, 164*
Parker, Clifford S., *21, 166*
Perlman, Michael, *30, 85, 164*
Porath, Yosef, *21, 166*

Price, James D., *3-5, 10-11, 25-26, 28, 31, 83, 165*
Revell, E. J., *15, 24-25, 97, 104-5, 163, 165, 167*
Seales, William B., *21, 166*
Segal, Michael, *21, 166*
Shor, Pnina, *21, 166*
Spanier, Arthur, *19, 28, 30, 166*
Spurling, Helen, *53, 166*
Stec, David, *53, 166*
Steiner, Richard C., *114, 166*
Tov, Emanuel, *21, 166*
van der Merwe, Christo H. J., *54, 79, 166*
Vanhoozer, Kevin J., *145, 166*
Waltke, Bruce K., *53, 71, 79, 166*
Weil, Daniel M., *28-29, 166*
Wickes, William, *3, 10, 15-19, 21, 23, 25-26, 28-31, 37-38, 50, 83, 89, 107, 110, 154, 167*
Williams, Ronald J., *79-80, 167*
Yardeni, Ada, *21, 166*
Yeivin, Israel, *3, 13, 15-16, 21, 23-26, 38, 70, 167*

SUBJECT INDEX

Accents (by name)
    Etnachta *2, 4, 9-10, 29, 33-52, 53-77, 79, 82-84, 86-93, 95, 98, 100-101, 105, 109, 119-23, 125, 128-33, 135, 137-42, 146, 149, 151*
    Siluq *35, 55, 68, 70, 82-83, 85-88, 91, 95, 97, 100-101, 151*
    Tipecha *51, 72, 82, 84-85, 88, 120, 138, 151*
    Zaqef *10, 46, 48-50, 55-58, 62-63, 65, 68-73, 76, 82, 84-85, 88-93, 97, 100-101, 110, 119-24, 136, 140, 151-52*

Accents (general)
    cantillation/chant *3, 9-10, 23, 26, 28-29, 30, 30, 149*
    dichotomy *3, 18, 25, 28-29, 31, 34, 37, 41*
    hierarchy *10-11, 17, 25-26, 29, 35, 38, 55, 72, 82-84, 111, 149, 151-54*
    pausal *24-25, 28-29, 46, 104-7, 111*
    subordination *25-26, 28-31, 35, 38, 48-49, 55, 57-61, 63, 68-69, 80, 82-86, 88, 93-94, 96, 109-10, 138, 147, 149, 154*

Accents (pattern)
    divergence *2, 6-8, 32, 33-34, 45-46, 48-52, 57, 62-72, 74-76, 81-82, 97-101, 104-10, 133, 138, 145-48*
    intentional pattern *2, 6-7, 32, 34, 37, 39, 44-45, 51-52, 55, 57, 60, 62, 70, 76, 81, 97, 104-5, 110, 119, 121, 124, 132-33, 137, 142-43, 145-48*
    nested phrases *30, 85-86, 89*
    stepping phrases *50, 84-86, 88-91, 94, 101*

Masoretes
    Aleppo Codex *12-13*, *15-16*, *20*, *102*, *161*, *164*
    ben-Asher *12-17*, *22*

Semantics/sense *1-2*, *3-12*, *19*, *24*, *26-29*, *31-32*, *34*, *37-38*, *47-50*, *52*, *58*, *61*, *63*, *67-68*, *72-77*, *79*, *100*, *109*, *114*, *123-26*, *128*, *131-33*, *137*, *142*, *145-49*

Syntax
    conditional *2*, *8*, *44*, *61*, *73*, *79-83*, *86-102*, *104-11*, *113*, *122-23*, *133*, *137-38*, *142*, *146-47*, *149*, *157-58*
    contrast *2*, *8*, *40-41*, *43*, *67-69*, *88*, *97-99*, *107-8*, *110*, *113-43*, *146-47*
    direct speech *2*, *7-8*, *33-52*, *53-54*, *57*, *59*, *61*, *63-68*, *70-71*, *73-75*, *80*, *88-90*, *93-94*, *105*, *109*, *113*, *122-23*, *126*, *133-37*, *142*, *146*
Text-hierarchy *38*, *87*
Ve'atah *2*, *8*, *53-76*, *113*, *146*, *149*

Scripture Index

Gen 3, *56*
Gen 4, *56*
Gen 11, *56*
Gen 12, *56*
Gen 13, *107-8, 111, 147*
Gen 15, *110, 121*
Gen 18, *2, 87, 96, 110*
Gen 20, *56*
Gen 21, *56, 110*
Gen 24, *56*
Gen 27, *56*
Gen 28, *2, 95-96, 121*
Gen 29, *9*
Gen 30, *56*
Gen 31, *56, 116*
Gen 32, *68-69, 75-76, 121, 146*
Gen 35, *121*
Gen 37, *56, 115*
Gen 41, *56*
Gen 44, *56*
Gen 45, *56*
Gen 47, *56*
Gen 48, *56, 121*
Gen 50, *56, 63-66, 73, 75-76, 146*

Exod 3 *56, 72, 74-76, 146*
Exod 4 *56*
Exod 5 *56*
Exod 9 *56, 121*
Exod 10 *56*
Exod 12, *93, 121*
Exod 19, *56*
Exod 23, *121*
Exod 32, *56*
Exod 33, *56*
Lev 21, *121*
Num 6, *130*
Num 10, *121*
Num 11, *56*
Num 14, *56, 121*
Num 22, *56*
Num 24, *56, 121*
Num 26, *121*
Num 31, *56*
Num 35, *105*
Deut 4, *56*
Deut 5, *56*
Deut 7, *93, 121*
Deut 10, *56*
Deut 12, *120-21, 123*
Deut 16, *121*

Deut 17, *131*
Deut 26, *56*
Deut 28, *12*
Deut 31, *56*
Josh 1, *56*
Josh 2, *56*
Josh 3, *56*
Josh 9, *56, 66, 75, 146*
Josh 13, *56*
Josh 14, *56*
Josh 17, *121*
Josh 22, *56*
Josh 23, *121*
Josh 24, *56*
Judg 1, *2, 35, 39, 41-43, 52, 64, 82, 84-86, 120, 123, 128-29, 141-43, 146-47*
Judg 2, *2, 35, 118, 120, 123, 125, 136-38, 142-43, 147*
Judg 3, *35, 40, 118, 120, 123*
Judg 4, *2, 35, 42-43, 52, 64, 67, 82, 87-88, 96, 118, 120, 137-38, 143, 146*
Judg 6, *2, 35, 38-39, 52, 56-57, 67, 72, 74-76, 82, 86-87, 96-99, 101-2, 110, 118, 120, 123, 146-48*

Judg 7, *2, 35, 44-45, 52, 56, 71, 82, 120, 123, 127, 133, 138, 142, 146-47*
Judg 8, *2, 35, 40-41, 52, 67, 82, 120, 123, 146*
Judg 9, *2, 35, 44, 56, 82, 90-92, 96, 99-102, 109-10, 120, 123, 137, 147-48*
Judg 10, *2, 35, 120, 123, 126, 142, 147-48*
Judg 11, *2, 35, 37, 44, 46-47, 52, 56-57, 64, 71, 82, 94-96, 118, 120, 123, 129-30, 133, 136, 138-39, 142-43, 146-48*
Judg 12, *35*
Judg 13, *2, 35, 56-59, 61, 76, 82, 92-94, 96, 100-101, 118, 120, 123, 139, 143, 146*
Judg 14, *2, 35, 56-57, 82, 88-89, 91, 96, 118, 120, 123, 130-31, 141-43, 147*
Judg 15, *2, 35, 39-41, 52, 56-57, 59, 76, 82, 120, 123, 135-36, 138, 143, 146*

SCRIPTURE INDEX   175

Judg 16, *35, 37, 48-50, 52, 67,*
   82, 97, 102-4, 120, 123,
   133-34, 138, 143, 146,
   148, 155-57
Judg 17, *35, 39, 43, 56-57,*
   65-66, 74-76, 146
Judg 18, *35, 56-57, 65-66,*
   75-76, 120-21, 123,
   146
Judg 19, *35, 37, 40, 50-52,*
   120, 123, 136, 146, 148
Judg 20, *35, 56, 120, 123, 132,*
   136, 140, 143
Judg 21, *35, 82, 100-101, 110,*
   120, 123, 131-32, 142,
   147-48
1 Sam 2, *56*
1 Sam 6, *56*
1 Sam 8, *56, 121*
1 Sam 9, *56-57, 60-61, 76, 146*
1 Sam 10, *56*
1 Sam 12, *56*
1 Sam 13, *56*
1 Sam 15, *56*
1 Sam 18, *56*
1 Sam 19, *56*
1 Sam 20, *56, 64, 73, 121*
1 Sam 21, *56, 121*
1 Sam 23, *56*
1 Sam 24, *56*
1 Sam 25, *56, 121*
1 Sam 26, *56*
1 Sam 28, *56*
1 Sam 29, *56*
2 Sam 2, *56*
2 Sam 3, *56*
2 Sam 4, *56*
2 Sam 5, *121*
2 Sam 7, *56*
2 Sam 12, *56*
2 Sam 13, *56, 64, 73, 121*
2 Sam 14, *56*
2 Sam 15, *56, 64, 73*
2 Sam 17, *56*
2 Sam 18, *56*
2 Sam 19, *56, 70-72, 75-76,*
   146
2 Sam 21, *121*
2 Sam 24, *56, 69-70, 75-76,*
   146
1 Kgs 1, *56*
1 Kgs 2, *56*
1 Kgs 3, *56*
1 Kgs 5, *56*
1 Kgs 8, *56, 121*
1 Kgs 10, *131*
1 Kgs 11, *131*
1 Kgs 12, *56*

1 Kgs 18, *56, 121*
1 Kgs 20, *105, 121*
1 Kgs 22, *56, 121*
2 Kgs 1, *56*
2 Kgs 3, *56*
2 Kgs 5, *56*
2 Kgs 7, *56-57, 61-62, 76, 146*
2 Kgs 9, *56*
2 Kgs 10, *56*
2 Kgs 12, *56*
2 Kgs 13, *56*

2 Kgs 14, *121*
2 Kgs 17, *121*
2 Kgs 18, *56*
2 Kgs 19, *56*
2 Kgs 23, *121*
Ezek 23, *100*
Hab 2, *105*
Mal 1, *105-6, 111, 147*
Neh 8, *149*
1 Chr 21, *69-70, 75-76, 146*

www.ingramcontent.com/pod-product-compliance
Lightning Source LLC
Chambersburg PA
CBHW050905160426
43194CB00011B/2293